# Essential Skills for Managers of Child-Centred Settings

Managers in child-centred settings need to be able to draw on a wide range of personal and professional skills to ensure that they are providing the best possible service. Now in its second edition, *Essential Skills for Managers of Child-Centred Settings* looks at how you can develop the key leadership skills needed to manage people to achieve excellent settings for children.

The authors outline ten 'essential skills' for leading and supporting those around you in your child-centred settings and offer sound advice so you can build your personal and professional skills and become a confident and assertive manager. With a balance of both accessible theory and practical application from a wide range of settings, this book explains management theory and will help you to develop the skills to:

- become a confident leader
- set clear aims and objectives for your setting
- manage your time effectively
- make decisions and implement change
- build and develop a team
- reflect on and develop practice
- deal with difficult situations and people.

This book also contains case studies and 'real-life' scenarios from managers undertaking training with the authors which will ensure you provide an excellent service in your setting. No manager or leader should be without this user-friendly guide!

**Shelly Newstead** is the founder of Common Threads, a social enterprise which supports practitioners across the UK and abroad who use playwork practice in their work with children. She has managed and developed a wide range of playwork and childcare settings and written a series of management skills training courses specifically for this field.

**Emma Isles-Buck** has worked as a trainer and manager in childcare and playwork for various local authorities, charities and in private training companies. She has been an assessor and external verifier for playwork NVQs, helped develop playwork qualifications for CACHE and developed several management courses and workshops for different client groups. Emma now works as a freelance project manager and writer.

# Essential Skills for Managers of Child-Centred Settings

## Second edition

## By Shelly Newstead and Emma Isles-Buck

Routledge
Taylor & Francis Group

LONDON AND NEW YORK

First published 2005
by David Fulton Publishers

This second edition published 2012
by Routledge
2 Park Square, Milton Park, Abingdon, Oxon OX14 4RN

Simultaneously published in the USA and Canada
by Routledge
711 Third Avenue, New York, NY 10017

*Routledge is an imprint of the Taylor & Francis Group, an informa business*

*British Library Cataloguing in Publication Data*
A catalogue record for this book is available from the British Library

*Library of Congress Cataloging in Publication Data*

Newstead, Shelly.

Essential skills for managers of child-centred settings / by Shelly Newstead and Emma Isles-Buck. – 2nd ed.

p. cm.

1. Child care services – Management. 2. Child care workers. I. Isles-Buck, Emma. II. Title.
HQ778.5.N48 2012
362.7 – dc22
2011008263

ISBN: 978-0-415-58553-8 (hbk)
ISBN: 978-0-415-58554-5 (pbk)
ISBN: 978-0-203-80501-5 (ebk)

Typeset in Bembo
by Saxon Graphics Ltd, Derby DE21 4SZ

# Contents

# Acknowledgements

Writing this book has been a culmination of experience gained through being managed ourselves by effective and ineffective managers, managing teams ourselves (both effectively and ineffectively!) and from working with others to overcome the management skills gaps in the sector. We would like to thank sincerely the following practitioners for their support in taking time to read and comment on the original manuscript: Maureen Smith, Anne Kelly, Verona Beaumont, Maria White, Beverly Webb and Sara Huggins.

Shelly and Emma would particularly like to thank all those who have taken part in management skills training courses with Common Threads or A Pair of Trainers. There are too many people to mention by name, but thanks to everybody for your enthusiasm and your honesty, and for letting us learn with you.

We would also like to thank family and friends for their enthusiasm and patience.

# Introduction

In the ten or so years since we first started writing this book, there have been huge changes in the field of working with children. There have been changes to legislation and the requirements for regulation and qualifications. Funding streams have come and gone, government policy has changed, national organisations have expanded and downsized, and local support structures have shifted. Different theories and ideas about good practice have been introduced and the increased use of the internet for finding and distributing information has made a huge difference to the way we think and learn.

So when the publishers asked us to do a second edition of this book, it felt like a bit of a daunting task to be honest! It was a case of 'so many changes and so little time' – where to start? We had lots of helpful suggestions – new qualifications, the Early Years Foundation Stage, the Playwork Principles, business planning and so on. However, apart from the fact that these things were all bound to move on at some point and render the book 'out of date' again pretty quickly, there was something else that didn't quite *feel* right about these suggestions. Eventually we were able to articulate what the problem was – these things are not 'universal', they are not things that all managers in our field need to know about, regardless of where and how they practice.

When we first set out to write a book for managers of what we termed 'child-centred settings', we wanted to write for all of those managers/deputies/room leaders we had met on our training courses for whom 'doing management' was one thing and 'being a manager' was something else. These people (and to some extent our own experience of management) had taught us that lots of people can 'do management' by learning how to write meeting notes, draw up a business plan, buy equipment and so on. These tasks might not be everybody's cup of tea, but there are generally standard ways of doing these things and once you've had a bit of practice, it feels like you've been doing them forever. However 'being' a manager requires of us something completely different to learning particular methods or set practices – and as the people on our courses told us, that's the scary bit.

Hersey (1984) summed up the challenge of management of child-centred settings as we see it: 'Management is working with and through others to accomplish organisational goals. Leadership is any attempt to influence the behaviour of another individual or group.' 'Doing' management in these terms means understanding what the job is and getting it done, working with others as and when the job requires it, and we do indeed see managers of child-centred settings as being the people responsible for making sure that the aim of the setting is achieved.

However, simply 'working with and through others to accomplish organisational goals' requires there to be some sort of stability in the workplace and for everybody to know what the job is and for that job to be relatively straightforward to achieve. In over fifty years of combined practice in this field, neither of us can honestly say that we have ever come across a setting where all of this applies at the same time! As we've already said, things change all the time in our field – in our settings as well as local and national levels – and we as managers have to constantly adapt both ourselves and our settings in order to be able to deliver the best possible service for children and families. This of course involves influencing the way that the people in our settings behave – both in their professional practice and sometimes also their personal behaviours whilst at work. So we see Hersey's definition of leadership as vitally important for management in our field, and in our experience this is the part that many managers struggle with.

When it comes to dealing with people, there are very few set formats or patterns to follow. In order to be able to respond to the variety of people, situations and problems they find themselves faced with on a daily basis, leaders have to rely on themselves and their own judgement and skills. These are the ten 'essential skills' that we have identified and chosen to write about in this book – skills which are not only essential for 'getting the job done' but also for leading and supporting people to do it with you. We believe that these skills will also help managers to 'do' management – all of the skills underpin standard management tasks that managers in our field will need to undertake (putting together a budget is impossible if you are unable to make clear decisions, for example), and you can learn more about the 'doing' side of management in many of the books listed in the further reading list at the back of this book.

So when we finally began this new edition, we asked ourselves whether the managers we had recently worked with were really any different to those we had worked with ten years ago, and whether those vital 'essential skills' had changed. Managers are still more likely to be promoted from within and are often highly-skilled practitioners rather than practiced managers, and this still causes a great deal of stress and anxiety. We still feel that in our field as long as everything continues to change around us, managers need to be able to draw on a foundation of personal and professional skills which enable them to enable their teams to develop and deliver really good services for children and families. So we hope that you find the revisions in this new edition useful and that the new 'First Person' case studies are helpful. These are all based on assessments and presentations given by managers on our training courses, and we are once again extremely grateful for our participants' willingness to honestly share their experiences of putting some of our ideas into practice.

We would very much like to hear how you have used this book and welcome comments and feedback – please email us at info@commonthreads.org.uk – we look forward to hearing from you!

## A few notes on language

We always wanted to write this book in a way that would support as many people as possible across the broad field of working with children, young people and families. To do this we have had to take a few 'shortcuts' with language, and so here are a few definitions to explain how we use specific terms in the book.

Management/leadership – we use the terms 'manager' and 'leader', or management and leadership interchangeably, as the working definition that we are guided by is that of Hersey (1984) as above. There are many debates about whether management and leadership are one and the same or part of each other, and you will find more ideas and definitions in some of the books listed in the further reading list.

Managers – when we use the word 'managers' in this book we mean anybody who works in a management or leadership role who has responsibility for all or part of the setting. In practice in our field this could also mean the owner, a deputy manager, a supervisor or room leader, a co-ordinator and any other job titles you can think of – we've even had childminders on our training courses who work on their own but have used these skills to work more effectively with other childminders, support colleagues or their own families! We also wanted to note that we have not made the assumption that all managers are paid – we've both done enough voluntary management posts to know this is definitely not the case! – so 'managers' can also refer to voluntary management committee members. Neither have we assumed that 'managers' are all supernumerary, as it is still the case that many people working in a management/leadership capacity will need to juggle this role with 'hands-on' work with children.

Child-centred setting/setting – whilst neither of us is particularly fond of the phrase 'child-centred', we originally settled on this phrase for the title of the book because we couldn't think of how else to incorporate the huge range of settings that we were writing for! So 'settings' means any place where children spend time being supervised by adults for the purposes of play and/or care and/or education. The sort of settings we had in mind when originally writing this book were after-school clubs, adventure playgrounds, playgroups, nurseries, open-access playschemes, crèches and so on. In the last few years we have been delighted to find out this list has been increased by our readers to include SureStart Centres, childminders, residential care, schools, social services, play ranger projects, local authority play services and lots more! These settings may be permanently set up or need to be packed away after each session, they may have separate office space or they may not and so on – we have tried to write this book so that the ideas can be adapted to the variety of spaces used.

Staff/team members/practitioners – we have used these terms to mean 'people you work with and probably have some responsibility towards'. This could of course include colleagues working on the same level and volunteers.

# Confidence

Some readers may be surprised to find confidence the first skill covered in this book. In the introduction we gave a definition of the role of the manager of a child-centred setting, and explained that managers need to be able to use leadership skills in order to influence others so that they will achieve the organisational goals. Any attempt to help others to change their behaviour requires confidence on the part of the manager.

## Essential skills for developing confidence

- Vision
- Self-esteem
- Assertiveness
- Long-term thinking
- Accepting compliments
- Staying present
- Accepting imperfection
- Sharing responsibility
- Being accountable.

## Why is confidence important for managers of child-centred settings?

There are two types of confidence that managers need when working in child-centred settings:

1. Confidence in the fact that it is indeed part of their role to influence the behaviour of others so that the setting is working towards its organisational aim and achieves the best possible quality of service for the children who attend.
2. Confidence in their own abilities to manage and lead others in the way that will help them to achieve their organisational aim.

It is important for managers, and those with whom they work, to understand that the role of the manager should be a *pro-active* role, not a *re-active* one. Very often managers in child-centred settings are seen as the person with whom the buck stops. Whilst it is, of course, true to say that taking ultimate responsibility is part of your role, a manager is not simply a trouble-shooter or an administrator. A manager also needs to be 'out there', taking a lead in shaping the sort of service the setting is delivering to the children you work with, and making sure that you are meeting all the expectations about how good your service should be. Chapter 2 looks at this area of a manager's role in more detail.

Not everybody understands this as a vital part of the role of a manager. Managers can often find themselves in situations where their own managers do not fulfil this role. Not only do they then not have a good role model to follow, but they also have to have enough confidence to be able to re-shape their role and to be accountable for that to their superiors. In some situations individual team members (or even whole teams) can find it difficult to accept their manager as somebody who will be focused on developing the setting and inevitably making changes to the way that people work. So managers in child-centred settings need a double dose of confidence: confidence in their own abilities to be able to be pro-active in their setting and to develop and shape the ways things are done, and enough confidence in their role to be able to explain to others that this is what their job is about.

Exuding confidence is not an option when we manage child-centred settings. No confidence, no leadership – and no leadership, no vision. The children you work with deserve the very best service you and your team can give them – and it's up to you to make sure that they get it. It is not possible to do it all yourself, and therefore you need to be able to manage others in a way that encourages them to do it with you – in other words, you need to be confident enough to be a leader.

Other chapters in this book will help you with specific skills, such as decision making, time management and giving feedback. But before you can acquire such skills, you need the confidence to believe that your role is about shaping, influencing and guiding, and that you have the ability to be able to achieve this.

So the person to start with is **you** and how you feel about your role right now.

# Developing your own skills

## Self-esteem

All of us need it, very few of us have enough of it. Good self-esteem is vital in being able to feel confident about your role as a manager, the decisions you make at work, and your ability to deal with awkward situations and difficult people. If you get out of bed in the morning thinking that you are a capable and competent person, looking forward confidently to the challenges that the day will bring, then congratulations! Your self-esteem is probably just about right. However, if you go to work worrying about that conversation you're going to have to have, the paperwork you dread completing or the telephone call you've been putting off making, then maybe you don't feel as good about your abilities to manage such situations satisfactorily, and maybe your self-esteem could do with a bit of a boost.

Low self-esteem can be due to the gap between what you perceive to be your ideal characteristics and what you feel the reality actually is. For example, you may feel that it is really important in life to be patient with others, but in reality you know that you have a bit of a short fuse. Many people spend their lives striving to fill this gap, rather than accepting that the gap exists. In doing so, they are focussing on something they perceive to be negative about themselves. The likelihood is that they will not be able to close the gap to their liking, and will therefore feel dissatisfied with themselves – or, in other words, suffer from low self-esteem.

This does not mean, of course, that most of us could not try to be a bit more patient, a bit more creative, a bit better with paperwork – whatever we would rather be. But the key to good self-esteem is to be able to notice the gap and to manage it, rather than trying to fill it, which inevitably leads to those feelings of being out of control and powerless. So instead of telling ourselves, 'I'm really bad at making decisions, and I must be more decisive', we need to treat ourselves a bit more gently. 'I'm not very confident about making decisions, and I would like to be, so I will do a few things to help me to develop more skills in decision making', is an approach that will help us to increase the skills gradually and build self-esteem rather than destroying it.

To have good self-esteem means feeling competent and capable in yourself – that you have the skills and abilities to cope with whatever comes your way. It is important to notice that in the vast majority of tricky situations, there is nobody telling you that you can't cope – except you. Dealing with difficult conversations with parents, for example, may not come easily to many of us, but people with good self-esteem will not dread these types of situation or put them off, because they know that they can handle them, however difficult it might be. Good self-esteem gives us confidence even when we may not feel confident, because whatever the situation, we will still feel at ease with ourselves afterwards.

## Assertiveness

It's one of those chicken-and-egg situations, isn't it? The more confidence we have, the more assertive we can be, and the more assertive we are, the more confident we feel!

It's important to remember that assertiveness is not the same as being aggressive. Some people seem to confuse an authoritarian style of behaviour with assertive behaviour, and the two are not the same at all. It is in fact more helpful to think of assertive behaviour as being 'quietly confident'. To put it another way, assertiveness is 'behaviour which helps us to communicate clearly and confidently our needs, wants and feelings to other people without in any way abusing their human rights' (Lindenfield, 1986). This may sound reasonably simple and straightforward, but there are several ways in which we avoid making our wants, needs and feelings known, such as:

- Using 'you' instead of 'I' in order to avoid taking responsibility for what we really think or feel. For example, 'You can tell that she's fed up because...' instead of 'I think she's fed up because...'

- Using phrases such as 'I wonder if' and 'would you mind' instead of making a direct request of a colleague

- Saying 'we' when we really do mean 'you'! For example, 'Could we try to keep the craft cupboard tidier so that we can find things?' instead of 'I would like you to keep the craft cupboard tidier so that you can find what you need'

- Using other peoples' perceived or imagined feelings and thoughts in a way that suggests that it is what everybody else thinks or feels instead of what you think or feel. For example, 'The rest of the team wants you to...' instead of 'I would prefer you to...'

It is very important for managers to be able to take responsibility for their own wants and feelings and to communicate those to others. Apart from ensuring that those wants and feelings are clearly communicated and unambiguous, such assertive behaviour also sets a good role model to follow and encourages others to also adopt assertive behaviour patterns. If you recognise any of the non-assertive phrases above as phrases which you would normally use, try to gradually introduce the phrases which start with 'I' instead. This may feel strange at first, but you should notice the difference in how much more confident using such phrases makes you sound and feel after a while.

Gael Lindenfield (1986) gives the following steps to follow in order to behave assertively:

- Decide what you want

- Decide if it is fair

- Ask clearly for it

- Do not be afraid of taking risks

- Be calm and relaxed

- Express your feelings openly

- Give and take compliments easily

- Give and take fair criticism.

Many of us would like to think that this is how we behave all the time, and some people do indeed behave assertively without having to think about it. However, it is quite a difficult skill to master. How many of us, for example, like to think that we take fair criticism, whereas in actual fact we are apt to become defensive and try to explain ourselves when somebody tells us about something we could do differently? Like any other skill, assertiveness is something many of us need to practice and continue to develop throughout our lives.

# Long term thinking

If you think your confidence does need a bit of a boost at the moment, it's not reasonable to expect that to happen overnight. Developing confidence takes a combination of experience, skills, knowledge and time. There are some publications listed in the further reading section at the end of this book that may help you to develop confidence in the longer term.

In the meantime, however, there's no reason why you can't appear more confident than you actually feel, and see if this makes a difference to how you feel and how other people feel about you. Here are some techniques to give your confidence short term boost. Practised over a period of time, these can also help confidence to develop in the long term:

## Smile

Yes, it's that easy – smiling really does make us feel better. It has another bonus, which is that it also makes other people feel better too! Smiling is a very useful technique when thinking about that self-esteem gap – it is quite difficult to feel nervous or worried about doing something if you are smiling.

## Walk like the manager, talk like a leader

Can people tell who the person with ultimate responsibility is in your setting? Not because you are the person bossing people around or the person with the loudest voice, but because you are the person who exudes confidence and inspires confidence in others around you. Develop that feeling of quiet confidence by 'walking tall' and looking like you're in control – and others will assume that you are in control too.

## See difficult situations as a series of stepping stones

Many people see difficult situations as a set of barriers or hurdles. If you change the way you approach such situations by envisaging a set of steps to help you to sort it out, you will feel your confidence levels rising as you take each step.

## Tackle first the things in your daily routine that knock your confidence

If you go into work dreading the difficult conversation you need to have, or working out ways of avoiding writing that report that you can't get your head round, make a decision that you will do that thing first (and stick to this decision!). By doing so you will probably find that it actually wasn't as difficult as you thought it was going to be, and you will get an instant confidence boost for the rest of the day.

# Accept compliments

Our confidence increases when we feel good about ourselves. We can help ourselves to feel good about ourselves by taking positive steps to increase our self-esteem. We can also allow others to further enhance our confidence by accepting compliments that other people pay us. For some reason, however, lots of us find this really difficult, and so we start saying things like, 'Oh, I don't really listen well/give positive feedback/understand the accounts', apparently in order to deny that the compliment is true. The other common response is to make a joke out of the compliment: 'Well, you've just caught me on a good day – you should have seen me in a mess with this yesterday!'

When somebody says something nice about something you've done, or a quality that you have, it is vital for your confidence levels to accept it gracefully. This means doing two things – first of all, say nothing but 'thank you'. Don't be tempted to enter into the 'Oh it was nothing' routine – somebody wants to pay you a compliment, so let them! The second thing you must do is to give yourself some credit. They really did want to acknowledge something good that they have noticed about you – it is very unlikely that they made up the compliment. Believe that you have done a good thing and give yourself a pat on the back!

## Staying in the present

Focus on what is going on at the present time. Don't worry about what might happen as a result of what you are saying and doing – put your energy into concentrating on what's happening in the here and now. The present is the only time you can do anything about. If you worry about what could happen, your confidence levels will drop as you waste energy agonizing about things that could go wrong but may never actually take place.

## Accept imperfection

Earlier we talked about the need to accept that we are not perfect as a way of developing our self-esteem. Very few people can be good at everything. We need to be able to accept that we are not perfect people in order to feel confident about ourselves.

Another important way in which we can contemplate accepting imperfection is to take on board that everybody makes mistakes. In our working lives we will make wrong decisions, we will misjudge situations, we will do things that we really could have done better. By and large, most of the things that we could have done differently will not be major disasters. We need to aim for 'good enough' outcomes to our actions, and be pleased when these happen, rather than aiming for perfection as our confidence levels will drop when we inevitably fail. Managers need to accept their own mistakes and use them to help develop their professional practice. Chapter 3 looks at ways of doing this. The key to maintaining confidence levels while learning from our mistakes is to approach professional mistakes professionally, rather than to see them as personal failures.

Managers also have to learn to accept imperfection in others as well as in themselves. We have talked so far in this book about the need for managers to act as leaders, which involves affecting the way that other people behave. It is perfectly acceptable to support people in making changes to their working practices in order to improve the service being offered in line with your organisational objectives. However, it is not realistic to expect to change the way that others think and act. Individuals can only change their own practice, and it is important to realise that nobody else can do it for them. Managers cannot hope to change people by the force of their will or their support, but must instead rely on people to make changes to their practice themselves. This can, of course, lead to a situation where there is not enough change in an individual for practice to improve, and it is then up to the manager to decide what level of imperfection can reasonably be accommodated in the setting.

## Sharing responsibility

Managers are, of course, ultimately responsible for what goes on in their setting. However, within this overall responsibility, there are many things that managers can support others in being responsible for. Managers in child-centred settings sometimes tend to take on too much responsibility – responsibility for how others feel and behave, for example. This is not to say, of course, that managers do not need to notice and to respond to other people's behaviour and feelings, but responding appropriately is different to taking responsibility for those things. It can also be the case that managers sometimes take inappropriate responsibility for parts of other people's jobs – managers in child-centred settings are often martyrs to the maxim, 'if you want a job doing, do it yourself'. They can often easily fill their day with things that other people haven't done, just because it is quicker to do it themselves than remind the person who should be doing it to get on with it. Not only does this mean that the manager cannot perform their own role of developing the service, but also it quite often means that they suffer from a lack of confidence, as they feel a sense of powerlessness in 'having' to cope with everything. Managers who develop the skill of sharing responsibility whenever appropriate feel their confidence increase as they realise that they are capable of effecting change in their setting.

## Being accountable

We use the phrase 'professional integrity' later in the book, and by this we mean accepting responsibility and accountability. It is very easy to blame things on others and to avoid looking honestly at our own part in situations that could have gone better. Confident managers do not try to avoid being held to account, and this acceptance of responsibility increases their confidence levels. This is because others respect them, and they also respect themselves, for being able to deal with the responsibility.

## First person – developing confidence

We always had a lot of unpaid fees. I really didn't like to make a fuss in case people took offence, so I usually just pleaded quietly! But this time I decided that I needed to be more confident in asking for fees to be paid, so I wrote letters which set out how much was owed, when I needed them to pay by and gave times to come and talk to me if there were problems with paying the bill. This turned out to be much more effective – out of four late payers, three settled by the 'due date' and one dad came in to playgroup – there were financial problems in the family and I've been able to give him some support in getting things sorted out.

Nursery Manager

## Putting it into practice

- Develop confidence in your role as somebody who should be leading and developing the work of your team.
- Improve your self-esteem to increase your confidence.
- Accept imperfection in yourself and others.
- Try to notice when your behaviour could be more assertive and practice assertiveness skills.
- Accept compliments from others with a smile instead of an excuse!
- Decide what your boundaries are and what other people need to take responsibility for.
- Accept that increasing confidence levels takes time and practice to achieve.

# Vision

As people who work with children, our jobs involve helping children to develop skills, knowledge and values. This may involve different things, depending on the setting – some may focus on social development, others educational development or physical well-being. Whatever the purpose, all settings should contribute to the present and future well-being of children in some way, shape or form.

When asked, many managers are able to describe how their setting plays an important part in children's development. However, this important work of child-centred settings is often taken for granted by those who work there. Settings rarely set out their vision for the children they work with in any meaningful way, but use instead bland descriptions of their services which sound like descriptions of similar settings across the land. This is unfortunate, as not only do these descriptions play down what the settings are achieving for children, they also hinder the management of the setting.

## Essential skills for developing vision

- Confidence
- Describing vision
- Setting clear aims and objectives
- Communicating vision.

## Why is vision important?

Vision can be described as the ability to think about the future in a positive, imaginative and creative way. In the context of working with children, vision is important for the following reasons:

1. To describe the benefits our work can offer to children in the short, medium and long term.
2. To describe the sort of goals the setting should work towards.
3. To make sure that day-to-day practice is in line with what we want to achieve for children in our setting.

Having a vision for the setting is vital, so that everybody knows why your setting exists and what it aims to achieve. Settings that do not have any sort of vision to work towards are in danger of becoming stale, and therefore not delivering the best possible service for the children. Managers need to be able to hold and develop a vision so that the rest of the team are constantly aware of what their work is about and why it is important to change and develop their practice. Working to achieve a vision improves the service for children, as well as keeping individual team members focused and motivated.

## First person – developing a vision

Coming from a sports background I'd organised our playscheme in a very structured way, with quite a lot of the sessions being more like coaching than play. Although nothing had ever been written down, the staff team had obviously 'caught' my vision, and were also working in a very programmed and adult-led way. Last year we had several comments from children which basically told us that they wanted more unstructured time with less adults bossing them around! So this year I organised a team discussion on what our vision for the six weeks should be, and we ended up talking about the fact that we were a *play*scheme and what this meant for the kids. We talked about practical things – like in coaching you are there to lead, but in play you are there to support and observe. By the time playscheme started we had a much clearer vision of what we were trying to achieve – and this was the first year that we allowed play fighting as a result!

Playscheme Leader

Managers in child-centred settings can sometimes feel that they are on some sort of never-ending treadmill – work life appears to be a perpetual cycle of planning, paperwork and problems. The 'doing' and the 'fun' of working with children can sometimes seem very remote. It is all too easy to get bogged down in the daily grind of administration, regulations and meetings and to lose touch with the reasons for working in this field in the first place.

One of the reasons that managers lose touch with the value of their work is because they cannot connect the day-to-day 'managing' of paper and people with the long-term benefits of the direct work with the children. They forget that, while they may not be providing direct input into the welfare and development of individual children on a daily basis, their role is just as crucial to their setting as that of anybody who does 'face-to-face' work. It is the manager's role to ensure that their whole setting is achieving the very best it can for the children who attend, and it is only the manager who can influence this in any meaningful, sustainable way. Whilst inspectors, development workers, trainers and others may help settings periodically, they cannot ensure that that setting is constantly monitoring and improving the way it delivers its vision for children. Only the manager, working regularly and consistently with their team, can make sure that children get the best service possible. When seen in this light, the role of the manager is transformed from the person with the shovel and the bucket to the person who plays the biggest part in making sure that the setting is making a difference to children's lives.

Vision is important then because it is closely tied in with motivation. If people know why they are doing something, and they can see the value of what they are doing, it is more likely they will perform better in order to achieve the task. For example, it is much easier to be motivated by the fact that you are ensuring the future of the setting by doing the funding application than it is to be motivated by the threat of your boss being cross with you if you miss the deadline. In day-to-day practice terms, it is possible to motivate people on even the most routine tasks if they can see the benefit to the children. Keeping the equipment cupboard tidy might be a tedious chore, but even this can be described in terms of the benefits that children will gain from a tidier cupboard. Of course, being motivated by vision doesn't work for everybody – we have to recognise that some team members are motivated by other things that have more to do with reward and personal achievement. However, being able to describe the value of practice in terms of benefits for the children does help people to understand the part that they play in helping children to develop.

## Personal and organisational vision

It is important to acknowledge that there are two types of vision – personal vision and organisational vision. In an ideal world, the personal vision of the manager is reflected in the organisational vision of the setting, and vice versa. However, there can be situations where the vision of the manager is different from that of the organisation for which they work.

For example, a manager who goes into playwork to pursue their vision about the value of free play for children could find themselves managing childcare provision. Both open access play provision and playcare settings have much to offer children and families, but they exist for different reasons and will therefore work towards different organisational goals.

Such a conflict can cause great difficulties, both for the individual concerned and for the organisation. Managers can suffer from stress as a result of their personal vision being in conflict with that of their organisation. Organisations can suffer from a manager managing towards a personal vision, as the organisation goes in one direction and the manager tries to go in another.

Sometimes managers need to accept such clashes of vision and work out strategies to help them to manage in spite of the conflict. At other times, it is fairer to everybody concerned for the manager to find another post where the values and vision of the organisation tie in more closely with their own.

## Describing vision

In the introduction to this book, we defined management as 'working with and through others to accomplish organisational goals' (Hersey, 1984).

This definition of course prompts the question: what are organisational goals?

As we said at the start of this chapter, different child–centred settings will have different reasons for existing. These may include, for example:

- helping children with educational achievement;
- enabling children to take part in a wide range of play opportunities;
- developing children's social skills and self-esteem;
- helping parents with parenting skills;
- community development objectives, such as crime prevention.

Whatever the motive for existing, each setting will have something unique to offer to children and their families. This intention, of offering some sort of service or support to children and/ or families, is what we mean by an organisational goal.

Organisational goals in child-centred settings should be visionary – that is, they should describe what the setting hopes to achieve for those who use it, rather than just describing the type of environment that they provide, or what you think you are already doing. It is also important to remember that even when child-centred settings are set up to make a profit, the vision for the children can and should still be described.

There are many terms for describing what a setting does and why it does it. The above definition uses the term 'organisational goals' and you will probably also be familiar with phrases such as mission statements, aims and objectives, operational plans, etc. We will concentrate on expressing the vision as a set of aims and objectives, as being able to develop clear aims and objectives is a very useful skill that can be used in many different areas of management.

## Setting clear aims and objectives

The place to start with aims and objectives is to understand the difference between the two. This difference can be defined as follows:

- An **aim** sets out what you are hoping to achieve, and therefore aims always start with the word '*to*'.
- **Objectives** spell out the way you are going to achieve your aim, and they therefore always start with '*by*'. Objectives are like the stepping-stones which get you to where you want to be. So whilst you would usually only have one aim which describes what you want to achieve, each aim can have as many objectives as it needs.

Once you have got your aim and objectives for your setting drafted out, you need to find out whether they are going to be useful to you as a manager; that is, whether you will be able to use them to lead and monitor the work of your setting. You can use a handy acronym to find out how useful they are – SMART (Doran, 1981), which stands for Specific, Measurable, Assignable, Realistic, and Time-related. Checking to see whether your aim and your objectives are SMART will help you to make sure that they are useful to you in managing your setting.

You should also find that your aim and objectives automatically become more visionary as they become clearer, more specific and measurable.

## Specific

You need to look at your aim and see whether it says exactly what it means – or is it a bit vague and woolly? For example, many child-centred settings have words like 'safe', 'happy', and 'secure' in their aim. Are these specific enough to help you to manage your setting – in other words, can you actually say what 'safety' means in the context of, for example, an after-school club which caters for 4–12 year olds? After all, what's safe in one set of circumstances will not be safe in others (and vice versa) – so can a word like 'safety' be used to describe accurately what a child-centred setting aims to achieve? And likewise with 'happy' – if some children are sad in a nursery, does this mean that the manager's job is to go round cheering everybody up in order to achieve the aim of the setting?

## Measurable

Will you be able to tell when you are getting close to achieving your aim and when it has been achieved? For example, in the case of words like 'safe' and 'happy', will you be able to measure these? It is, in fact, very difficult to measure an aim or part of an aim that is not specific. If your aim cannot be measured, then it is not going to help you to manage your setting – because if you can't tell if you're achieving your aim, then you might as well not have one! When thinking about whether an aim is measurable or not, we also need to think about the methods which will be used to measure it. If you can't think of ways to measure what you are hoping to achieve, then it probably isn't measurable!

## Assignable

'Assignable' means that you need to be clear about who will carry out the work required to achieve them. You also need to make sure that you are clear about who is responsible for making sure that they are achieved. Often this will be the same person who is doing the work, but sometimes there will be a different person responsible for making sure that the job gets done. For example, if you want the whole team in a baby room in a nursery to implement a new routine, it will be the room leader who will be 'assigned' to make sure that the whole team is trained and supported in achieving the change. When assigning aims and objectives, it's important to be realistic about the amount of time it will take over and above that person's existing workload, and also to think about the skills and knowledge that the person needs to be able to achieve them. Remember too that you need to be specific in setting your aims and objectives, so don't be tempted just to write 'everyone' as a way of assigning them. When more than one person is involved, make a list of the individual names as this will help you to think about the workload and expertise of everybody involved.

# Realistic

All aims and objectives need to be realistic, which means that there needs to be a very good chance that you can achieve them. Think about whether you have the relevant expertise, enough resources, the right knowledge and have allowed enough time for them to be achieved. It's good to have aims which give you something to work towards, but it's stressful and de-motivating to have objectives which mean that you will never get there!

# Time-related

Aims and objectives should normally state when you want to achieve them by. This gives you a date or a time to aim for and to check against to see if you are on track. However, in the case of an organisational aim, it would only be useful to put a time limit on the aim or the objectives if your setting operates on a short-term or time-limited basis (for example, a summer holiday playscheme or a one-year funded parent and toddler group).

## Case study

Jo, the manager at Dun'playin Playcentre, decided to revisit their organisational aim and objectives. She couldn't really remember what the aim and objectives were, so she went to dig them out of a file. They read as follows:

> The playworkers of Dun'playin Playcentre are committed to providing an environment which meets the needs of all children. Our overriding aim is to create a safe and caring environment where every child can enjoy themselves in a happy, friendly atmosphere.

Jo settled down with the SMART checklist to take a long hard and honest look at whether this aim helped her to manage the playcentre.

The first thing that she noticed was that there was nothing in the aim about play. 'Odd, that, given that we're a playcentre', she thought, and made a note. She also looked at the phrase about meeting the needs of all children. 'Is that realistic?' she wondered, 'and it doesn't say what needs we want to meet, so it's definitely not specific.' Jo pondered for a while about the word 'caring' – after all, what's 'caring' on the part of a parent is different to the way that playworkers care for children. 'Maybe that isn't specific enough – just like 'safe' is rather vague. After all, we've got a twelve-foot climbing tower in the yard – that couldn't really be described as 100 per cent safe but the kids get so much out of it we certainly wouldn't want to take it down.' She also looked at the idea in the aim of children enjoying themselves, and realised that they didn't always actually want to enjoy themselves. 'Sometimes they come here to let off steam, sometimes they want to moan about their teachers or their parents, sometimes they just want to sit and do nothing and then go home again – and all of that's OK, although I wouldn't class any of that as "enjoying themselves" particularly', she thought.

Jo's SMART checklist looked like this:

- Specific – caring, safe, happy, friendly can all be interpreted in different ways and therefore are not specific enough. Play isn't mentioned and should be.
- Measurable – you can't measure whether we are meeting the needs of all children! Safe, caring, etc are also not measurable.
- Assignable – we've only talked about the playworkers, not mentioned the volunteers or the management committee.
- Realistic – we simply can't meet all the needs of all children, and it's not realistic to want children to enjoy themselves or be happy all the time!
- Time-related – this one doesn't apply as we operate all year and are funded by the local authority (hopefully!).

Once she had finished her SMART checklist, Jo realised that she would either have to manage the playcentre in a very different way in order to meet this aim, or she would have to re-write the aim in order to reflect exactly what the playcentre was there to do. She could see from the exercise that the existing aim did not help her to manage the centre, and that if she did try to use it then it would actually get in the way of the work that the centre was trying to achieve. Jo therefore decided to rewrite the organisational aim, trying to make it SMART as she went, and this is what she came up with:

'Dun'playin Playcentre aims to meet the play needs of all children.'

'Well, it's certainly short and sweet', thought Jo, 'but is it SMART?'

S   – it is specific as far as it goes, but it doesn't say which children, so it could be more specific

M   – it is measurable, because we can assess play needs using some of the play theory and how we do this can go into our objectives

A   – it now talks about the work of the centre as a whole, so it's assigned to everybody who is part of the centre

R   – it is realistic as children are free to make their own choices about their play here and we try to support all children as and when they need us to do so

T   – it doesn't need to be time-related, but some of the objectives might need to be.

Jo then tweaked the aim in the light of this SMART exercise and added the objectives, which she also made SMART. By the time she'd finished, the aim and objectives read like this:

# Aim

Dun'playin Playcentre aims to meet the play needs of all children between the ages of 5 and 15 years from the Downs Estate.

## Objectives

We will do this by:

- continuously assessing the play needs of the children attending;
- responding to these play needs by ensuring that appropriate play types and materials are available at all times;
- providing support to individual children when required;
- providing support to groups of children when required;
- ensuring that fees are kept at a minimum to enable full access.

When she had finished, Jo decided that managing the playcentre according to this set of aims and objectives was going to be a lot easier. Now she could see what she was supposed to be managing, and, just as importantly, her team would be able to see clearly what they were supposed to be doing. 'To be fair,' Jo reflected, 'we are doing quite a lot of this anyway, but perhaps not in such a structured way as we could do. We'll need to work out the details now – how we assess and record play needs, for example. Perhaps I could turn each objective into another set of aims and objectives – that would help me work out how to achieve each one.'

Jo could see that her objectives should all add up to show how the aim was going to be achieved, and, in the same way, each objective could be turned into an aim by itself with its own set of objectives to show how the staff team could achieve it. In this way, the team would all have a shared vision of what their jobs were achieving for children, which they hadn't really had before.

## Communicating vision

Once the organisational aim is clear and SMART, it is important not to put it back in the file and forget about it. A set of organisational aims and objectives are incredibly useful management tools – not only for managers themselves, but also so that team members understand how the setting should operate. An organisational aim should therefore be a living document, which is used and reviewed as a part of everyday practice. Here are just some of the ways in which you can communicate your organisational aim:

- Use it when evaluating pieces of work or the work of your whole setting (see Chapter 10).
- Make sure that you make reference to it in team meetings, committee meetings etc.
- Remind yourself of what the aim of the setting is each week.
- Put it on the wall/notice boards.
- Include it in all leaflets and publicity.
- Make sure that every policy clearly states the aim and says how you will achieve it.
- Ask the children if they think that the aim is being achieved.

# Putting it into practice

- If you're not already sure, find out what the vision for your setting is.

- Try to describe this vision in terms of benefit for the children as accurately as possible.

- Make sure that your organisational aim reflects the vision of the setting.

- Use SMART to ensure that your organisational aim will help you to manage your setting according to the vision.

- Use every opportunity to communicate the organisational aim to others, both inside and outside your organisation.

- Be prepared to adapt or change the organisational aim if and when it no longer reflects the up-to-date vision for your setting.

# CHAPTER 3

# Reflective practice

Managers in child-centred settings may already be familiar with the term 'reflective practice' in the context of face-to-face work with children. Reflective practice can generally be described as a tool for self-evaluation, in that it enables us to learn from our achievements and our mistakes through assessing our own practice.

This chapter focuses on reflective practice as a technique which helps us to learn from our part in interactions with other people, as these interactions play such a large part in the role of a manager in a child-centred setting. Many other areas of work can be monitored and evaluated by using the techniques described later in this book. However, it is difficult to evaluate our interactions with others in the same way, as there are very few prescribed ways in which we can behave in order to achieve a certain outcome to an interaction. There are so many variables in human behaviour that trying to use methods normally used to evaluate situations where pre-determined models exist becomes meaningless. Reflective practice, however, can help us to evaluate our interactions with others in terms of:

- what we do
- how we do it
- why we do it that way
- whether we should do it that way in the future.

## Essential skills for developing reflective practice

- Confidence
- Staying in the present
- Accepting imperfection
- Honesty
- Flexibility
- Acknowledging personal success
- Professional integrity

- Analytical thinking
- Recognising barriers to reflective practice.

# Why is reflective practice important?

## 1. Reflective practice helps us to develop solutions to problems

Reflective practice stops us looking for answers where none exist. Managers are often keen to know 'how to deal with' the team member/parent/management committee member who is causing them strife. However, there are no 'templates' for the huge range of interactions which managers in child-centred settings deal with – there are only approaches and solutions. Interacting with different people at different times will produce different results. When you add into the equation that managers are people too, then we can see that any hope of 'getting it right' all the time is just not realistic.

Being a reflective practitioner means that we are able to start from a different point. Instead of asking, for example, 'I need to know how to stop children fighting', the reflective practitioner is able to draw on their experiences and their knowledge and ask, 'What have I learnt in other situations that might help me in situations where children fight?' Because, of course, there is no one way to 'stop children fighting' – there are only different approaches and interventions which face-to-face workers can try.

## 2. Reflective practice saves us time and energy

Using reflective practice gives shape and consistency to what can appear to be a separate set of experiences. It helps us to learn from these apparently unconnected experiences by giving us a means of drawing on the behaviours and the actions we have used in other circumstances. Reflective practice gives us a structure from which to develop what we have learnt so that we can use this knowledge again, rather than having to start from scratch every time.

Managers of child-centred settings who are reflective practitioners don't need to bash their heads against a brick wall until 'the answer' appears to questions such as 'How can I get Mrs Bloggs to turn up for work on time?' Reflective practitioners know that looking for 'the answer' is a waste of time and precious energy. They ask instead 'What can I use from other similar circumstances that I could try with Mrs Bloggs to get her to come to work on time?' Rather than waiting for the answer to appear, managers who are reflective practitioners get on with the job of developing different approaches to the problem based on their previous knowledge and experience.

## 3. Reflective practice helps us to develop our own practice

By using reflective practice we can start to make connections between what we wanted to achieve from our interactions and the part we played. This means that we can develop our own practice from apparently small events in our working lives. This makes reflective practice a particularly useful learning tool for managers in child-centred settings, as they often do not get feedback from others on their own practice (see Chapter 5 for more on giving feedback). There are several ways that managers of child-centred settings could get further support for developing their own reflective practice. These include:

- discussions with your own manager;
- finding a colleague from a similar setting who has the same sort of responsibilities as you;
- talking to a colleague from within the field but with a different job role; for example, a development worker;
- setting up a group of like-minded managers in your area to meet on a regular basis;
- joining a web-based discussion group.

## 4. Reflective practice is good practice

It is now considered good practice for everybody working in child-centred settings to make use of reflective practice as part of their continuing professional development and the development of the setting in which they work. If managers want to encourage the effective use of reflective practice across their setting, one way to do this is to lead the team by doing it themselves.

## 5. Reflective practice helps us to check theory against practice

Using reflective practice can provide us with a useful 'reality check'. It helps us to ensure that we are acting in the way that we believe we are acting. The field of working with children is awash with jargon which purports to describe the way we work. Phrases such as 'child-centred' and 'quality care' are now part of accepted professional terminology. Yet we do need to ensure that we are actually putting the words into practice. By thinking about the way in which we behave while working with others, the way we talk to parents, the way we play with children, the way we act in team meetings etc, we can discover whether we really are working in the way that we intended and in the way the standards of our setting require us to work.

## Specific and continuous reflective practice

It is useful to be able to think about two types of reflective practice when working in child-centred settings. Firstly, reflective practice can be a one-off analysis of a particular interaction and we describe this as specific reflective practice. This type of reflective practice can be used on a daily basis to look at how specific interactions have taken place. It is also often used as a development tool on training courses to help participants to 'think about a time when...' and to re-consider how they would now act in a similar situation in the light of new knowledge or skills gained on the course. Managers can use specific reflective practice in team meetings and supervision sessions as a technique to encourage others to think about their own behaviour in certain situations.

Secondly, the term reflective practice is also increasingly used to describe a way in which professionals who work with children are encouraged to behave all the time, rather than simply reflecting on isolated events. The phrase 'reflective practitioner' is often used to mean somebody who continuously uses reflection as a way of monitoring their own interaction with others – in other words, they are constantly aware of their thoughts and actions and the impact that these may have on others.

Managers who use continuous reflective practice develop something like a 'sound track' in their heads that provides a running commentary on what they are doing. Whilst they are talking going from one room of the nursery to the other, they think to themselves, 'How have I just walked through that room? Did I smile? Did I take time to comment on good practice? Or did I just rush through and ask somebody briefly to keep the room a bit tidier?' In continuous reflective practice, it is possible for the analysis and the development to happen all at the same time. In the scenario above, for example, an experienced reflective practitioner would be able to analyse their actions and make the necessary changes whilst they are walking through the next room. This type of reflective practice is therefore referred to in this chapter as 'continuous reflective practice'.

## Case study

Stuart loved his job as a manager of a playcentre. He was enthusiastic about helping the children to feel that the centre was for them, and spent a lot of time talking to the volunteers and staff who worked there about the importance of involving the children in the running of the setting.

At the beginning of December, Stuart decided that they would decorate the centre for Christmas. At the start of one of the sessions he brought in a large Christmas tree and the children got very excited. One girl asked Stuart where the Christmas tree was going to stand, and Stuart told her that he was going to put it in the corner of the room. After doing this, he got out some tree decorations, and organised the children to decorate the tree by giving out the decorations and telling them where to hang each one on the tree.

Stuart could have used continuous reflective practice to be aware of his actions during the activity, or he could have undertaken a piece of specific reflective practice after the event. Using either type of reflective practice, he would have noticed that his intention (of helping children to feel that the centre was theirs) did not match up with the outcome of the activity.

## Five-stage reflective practice model

In order for reflective practice to be a useful learning tool, it needs to be carried out in a structured way. Giving a shape to our reflection helps us to understand exactly what it is that we are learning. For example, it is very difficult to learn from an interaction by simply telling ourselves that it went well. We need to be able to identify why it went well and what we did that helped that particular situation. There are five stages in our reflective practice model:

intention, experience, actions, outcome, and development. Both continuous and specific reflective practice need to include all five stages. Remember that for continuous reflective practice, we will need to assess the situation as it is taking place. For specific reflective practice, the model should be applied after the event.

## 1. Intention

First of all we need to reflect on the original purpose of the interaction. What are we (or were we) aiming to achieve by our part in the interaction? In the case study above, Stuart was keen to help the children to feel like it was 'their' centre.

## 2. Experience

Then we need to reflect on what actually happened and gather together a factual account of what took place before, during and/or after the interaction. Stuart would have noted that he made the decisions about where the tree went and how it was decorated.

## 3. Actions

The next stage involves noticing our actions during the interaction – what we said, felt, thought, etc. We need to take care to notice what actually took place, not what we would have liked to have happened. Stuart might have noticed that he was in a bit of a hurry during that session and that he had told the children what to do rather than taking the time to help the children to make the decisions for themselves.

## 4. Outcome

We then need to assess the outcome of the interaction. Did it achieve, or is it achieving, what was originally intended? Again, honesty is vital here. Stuart would have noted that the tree got put up, but the children probably wouldn't have felt very involved in the process.

## 5. Development

Finally, what can be learnt from our part in the interaction? If it is achieving or has achieved its intended outcome, how did we act in order to help this to happen? If the intended outcome wasn't achieved, how could we have behaved differently in order to change the outcome of the situation? Stuart could take more time next time to involve the children and talk to them differently, by asking questions instead of giving them directions.

## First person – building reflective practice

I organised a behaviour course for our whole playscheme team, who had been working together for a couple of summers but had never really got the 'behaviour thing' right. I did the course with them, and during the day it became very obvious that everybody had very different ideas and opinions about 'behaviour'. It really did highlight the fact that our current approach to behaviour wasn't consistent, as what might be acceptable to some of the team was not acceptable to others. So straight after the course I arranged for a team meeting so that we could do some reflective practice to try to put what we had learnt into practice this time round. Instead of starting with the usual question about 'behaviour', I asked the team what sort of playscheme they wanted for the kids and used the reflective practice model to guide the discussion from there. By the end of the meeting we had agreed that what we wanted was a happy summer ('intention'); that our 'experience' of the last couple of years was that they could have been happier; that we'd learnt from the training that some of our 'actions' may have contributed to this (for example, two members of staff telling children off for the same thing at different times); and the 'outcome' of these actions were that children got confused and frustrated with us. We agreed that this summer we would all stick to the behaviour guidelines and leave our own opinions to one side ('development'), however hard that was for us to do!

Adventure playground Manager

# Developing your own skills

## Staying in the present

It is very difficult for people who are too stressed, tired, anxious, afraid, and so on, to carry out reflective practice effectively. This is because they either simply do not have the energy to stay focused in the present moment, or because their mind is whirring away with many different things and they are just too distracted to notice what they are doing and how they are doing it. Managers of child-centred settings need to be able to focus on what they are saying and doing in the here and now.

## Acceptance of imperfection

As we said in Chapter 1, perfectionists give themselves a really hard time because they find it difficult to get to grips with the fact that they are not perfect and neither are people they work with. One of the assumptions that lie behind the process of reflective practice is that sometimes we do get interactions with others right and sometimes we don't. Mastering the skill of reflective practice relies not only on understanding this assumption, but also accepting it and really taking it to heart. Making mistakes is part of the learning and development process – it is not a sign of personal weakness or failure.

# Honesty

Generally speaking, people who work in child-centred settings like to think they're doing a good job. Reflective practice sometimes makes us notice that we haven't acted in the way that we would have liked to have acted. Some people can find this quite painful, but the thing to remember here is that it is a learning experience. Being able to tap into what we really felt and thought about a situation is an invaluable experience. We cannot learn by putting up barriers in our own minds or by pretending that things are not as they are. The majority of situations where things haven't gone as you would have liked can be sorted out. Experiencing some sort of discomfort is a sign that you have noticed that things could be done better. It means that you have stayed open to the possibility of other ways of doing things, and that in the future you will be able to learn again. This is good news for the people that you manage and it is good news for the children in your setting – it means that your setting will benefit from you being honest enough to develop your own practice.

# Flexibility

Reflective practitioners are people who are open to the possibility of personal change. There is no point in analysing situations and thinking about how you might do them differently if you are resistant to changing your own behaviour. Things change – people change and what's considered good practice also changes. Part of a manager's role is to ensure that their setting delivers best current practice, and by using reflective practice we can consider whether our practice is as it should be. Changes in practice will very often mean changes in the way we need to act, and this is, after all, part of our professional development.

# Acknowledging personal success

It is important to remember that reflective practice is as much about what goes right as what could have gone better. As we mentioned in Chapter 1, many people are embarrassed to receive compliments from others. Even stranger perhaps is the fact that many people also find it hard to pay themselves compliments – these people seem to focus on the things that haven't gone so well and pay no attention to their achievements. Reflective practitioners give themselves a pat on the back for stuff that goes well, and when things don't go so well they give themselves credit for being brave enough to admit it.

# Professional integrity

It is all too easy to take things personally, especially when working with people. People who work in child-centred settings often take great pride and personal satisfaction in their work. It is no wonder then that many of us find it difficult not to take things to heart. Recognising the need to do things differently next time does not make you a bad person – it simply means that you have been professional enough to be able to make an objective assessment of your own behaviour.

## Analytical thinking

People working in child-centred settings are often very busy people. Managers of these settings have many different calls on their time and will often be called upon to make those 'on the hoof' decisions. Analytic thinking can be very difficult in this sort of environment, yet managers do need to be able to think in a structured way in order to develop their own practice and the work of the setting. Using models such as the five-stage reflective practice model can help to focus thinking in a structured way.

## Recognising barriers to reflective practice

Some people find reflective practice easy and others have to work a bit harder at it. This is simply because different people have different ways of thinking, learning and processing information. Those of us to whom reflective practice does not come so easily need to treat it just like another skill to be learnt as part of our management role and one which will take time and practice in order to develop fully. People can certainly learn to become reflective practitioners, but sometimes when things appear tough or challenging we can put up barriers in order to ward off change. So it is important to recognise and deal with the barriers in order to develop reflective practice. Some of the most common barriers we've come across are these:

- 'I'm a do-er, not a thinker'.
- 'I've been doing this job for 15 years and there's nothing you can tell me about running a nursery/playgroup/after-school club, etc'.
- 'But I've got enough to do already'.
- 'We're fine/I'm fine/My setting's fine as it is. Nobody has ever told me we're/I'm not/it isn't!'.
- 'I just get on with it – analysing it spoils it for me'.

## Case study

Denise is a manager of a nursery. Recently she has had some students working in her setting, and she has found herself becoming increasingly frustrated with the amount of time she has been spending supporting them. The final straw came one day when she asked one of the students to 'wash the dishes' after lunch, and, on returning from a meeting, found that he had done just that. All the dishes were spotless, but the cutlery and cups were still dirty and the kitchen had not been left clean and tidy.

Denise realised that she had been gradually losing her ability to deal with issues in the nursery calmly, so she decided to shut herself away and do a piece of specific reflective practice on this situation. This is what she came up with.

## 1. Intention

Denise knew that by asking the student to 'wash the dishes', she had meant for him to wash up all the equipment the children had used at lunchtime and to leave the kitchen clean and tidy.

## 2. Experience

Denise recalled that she had asked the student to carry out the task whilst she was in a hurry to get to her meeting.

## 3. Action

Denise noticed that when she was talking to the student, she didn't give him any opportunity to ask any questions and she didn't check what he had actually understood her to mean. She had made an assumption that everybody understood the meaning of the phrase that she used.

## 4. Outcome

What had actually happened, much to Denise's frustration, was that the dishes had been washed but the job was not completed.

## 5. Development

Denise resolved that, before asking people to carry out tasks again, she would not assume that they knew how to do the job. She would give clearer instructions first and also ask if there was anything else that the person needed to know before she left them to get on with it. She also decided to allow more time for setting tasks rather than doing it in a rush. She also decided that there was no point in getting frustrated with the student – she would instead use this as a training opportunity to show him how she wanted the task to be completed.

# Putting it into practice

- See reflective practice as a vital part of both your own role and of all the members of your team.
- After doing something that involved some sort of interaction with another person, take just three minutes to think about it before rushing onto the next thing.
- Develop continuous reflective practice by focussing on the interaction which is taking place and noticing what is happening.
- Use the five-stage reflective practice model to focus your reflective practice.
- Put aside time for specific reflective practice at the end of a shift, day or session.

- Encourage others to develop their reflective practice by role-modelling the techniques and introducing them into team meetings, supervision, etc.

- Find ways of getting support to develop your own reflective practice.

- Give yourself credit when you are pleased with the results of your reflective practice.

- When reflective practice shows you how you could behave differently next time, remember to accept the learning.

# CHAPTER 4

# Decision-making

Making a decision simply means choosing a course of action between two or more alternatives. This is an everyday part of working in child-centred settings and very often we make decisions without noticing that we are doing so. Practitioners in our field can often be heard talking about 'thinking on our feet', meaning that they have very little time to weigh up the alternatives before making a decision. Managers of child-centred settings are responsible for taking all sorts of decisions, and whilst some of these will be easily made, others will not. Managers therefore need to develop skills to help them to feel comfortable about making decisions as part of their role.

## Essential skills for decision-making

- Confidence
- Time management
- Accepting responsibility
- Professional integrity
- Intuition
- Reflective practice.

## Why is decision-making an important skill?

There are some managers who find decision-making difficult and regard it as an unwelcome chore rather than an integral and essential part of their job. These managers will put decisions off until it is actually far too late to make them properly, and because they haven't allowed enough time to make decisions, the decisions they do make are usually not very good ones. It is not a coincidence then that the next time they have to make a decision they do not feel very positive about having to do it!

Reasons for not liking decision-making include:

- fear of failure, not wanting to 'get it wrong';
- feeling stressed about having to make decisions within a certain time frame;

- seeing decision-making as having to 'take sides' and worrying about upsetting people;
- perceiving it as 'waste of time' to use a decision-making process rather than go with 'gut feeling'.

However we feel about it, being able to make decisions is a crucial skill for managers who are developing the work of their setting. Without clear decisions, teams will be unclear as to the direction that they are to work in and progress will therefore be slow or non-existent. Misunderstandings can also arise from situations where decisions have been ambiguous, with people getting frustrated because they cannot fully understand the implications of the decision. This can cause tension between individuals and within teams. Frustration can also be caused when too much time is taken over decisions, as other people are very often affected by decision-making and need to know the outcome so that they can put it into practice. Tension and frustration of any kind hamper the work and mean that managers have to use precious time and energy sorting out problems within their team, rather than taking the work of the organisation forward. A lack of any sort of decision-making can also mean that the setting becomes stuck in a rut. Making clear decisions in good time is therefore crucial to individuals and teams being able to achieve their organisational goal.

## Types of decisions

There are three different types of decisions that managers in child-centred settings are responsible for making. These are day-to-day decisions, operational decisions and development decisions. All of these types require a slightly different approach and set of skills.

## Day-to-day practice decisions

These are decisions that need to be taken on most days that the setting is operating. For example, decisions about whether a sick child needs to go home, if the bins need emptying, whether the rope swing is safe enough until it can be repaired, etc. To make these decisions, managers need a sound knowledge of the setting's policies and procedures, some successful experience in making such judgements, and a bit of faith in their own abilities to make those decisions. In the case of day-to-day practice decisions we go through a simple process, sometimes without even realising it, which is:

- establishing the facts
- weighing up the options
- deciding on the course of action.

Effective managers try to delegate as many of these day-to-day practice decisions to other members of the team. Unless your team is very small, there is usually somebody else who, with a bit of support and training, could make decisions about when to order more craft materials and whether it's necessary to bring children inside on a cold winter's evening. By delegating such routine, predictable decisions, managers free up more time to make the more involved decisions that they are responsible for.

# Operational decisions

These are the decisions that affect the quality of practice and provision within the setting; for example, judgements about whether a particular training course is suitable for volunteers, how much of the budget can be spent on replacing new play equipment, which sort of quality assurance scheme is most suitable for the setting, and so on. These decisions can only really be taken by the manager of the setting, who will need to refer to the operational policies and procedures and other documentation in order to make a decision in the best interest of the setting.

There will usually be some parameters involved in operational decisions – in other words, some sort of boundaries within which the manager needs to decide. In the examples above, the parameter for the training course is the content of the course itself; the parameter for replacing the play equipment is the amount of money in the budget; and the parameter for the quality assurance scheme is the content and process of the quality assurance scheme plus factors like cost, time involved etc.

It could be said therefore that operational decisions are relatively easy to make – there are usually a limited number of options with clear parameters. Again, knowledge, experience and confidence in their decision-making abilities will help managers to be able to make this sort of decision with relative ease.

# Development Decisions

In contrast to operational decisions, development decisions are those that are more complicated, more involved and usually have no previous examples, models, policies, etc to follow. There is nothing predictable about development decisions – they are not the sort of decisions that managers have to make every day, and when they do need to be made it is usually up to the manager to set their own parameters. Development decisions are those which will usually result in a major change for the setting and/or the service, and could include for example:

- whether to take on or lay off staff;
- whether to develop the outdoor space and, if so, how;
- whether to offer student placements and practice teaching;
- whether to take on registered charity status;
- whether to change the setting's operating hours;
- whether to open another branch of the service.

Some of these examples will, of course, have a precedent. Yet even if this is not the first time that staff have been taken on, the people involved in making the decisions may not be able to draw on previous experience as circumstances may have changed. Managers may therefore need to start 'from scratch', and later in this chapter we will look at a seven-step model which will help you to do that in a logical way.

Managers in child-centred settings need to focus on operational and developmental decisions. It is up to the manager to develop the service, and the ability to make those sorts of decisions is one of the things that differentiate managers from non-managers. Managers should take care that they are not just focussing on the day-to-day practice decisions, because it is too easy to get caught up in the daily routine and not actually manage and develop the service.

---

## Case study (Part 1)

Conrad manages a playbus. Last summer the playbus visited some rural areas and ran some free play sessions which included children of all ages. The feedback from the children was excellent, and so now they are preparing to run the same sort of sessions again this summer. However, external agencies (some of whom provide funding) are putting pressure on the playbus team to make the sessions more structured and to contain some holiday literacy support. Conrad and the rest of his team feel instinctively that the sessions wouldn't go down so well, and Conrad has to make a decision about how to go forward with the summer project.

Conrad has several options. He can:

- go with his and his team's gut feelings, ignore the pressure and carry on with the free play sessions;
- strike a compromise and run mornings as free play and afternoons as literacy support;
- turn the whole project into a literacy support scheme.

Conrad doesn't feel comfortable with any of those options and realises that he needs to put some time aside to make this decision.

(To be continued after the next section.)

---

## Seven steps to effective decision-making

Decision-making is best approached as an organised and logical thought process. The more we practice planned and organised decision-making, the easier it becomes. These seven steps are useful in helping us to think about operational decisions and developmental decisions clearly and logically. Remember that we are not suggesting that you use this process for day-to-day practice decisions – nobody would go through this to make a decision about whether the bins need emptying!

### 1. Define the parameters

There are two parameters that managers need to be clear about when setting out to make a decision. First of all, it is useful to remind yourself about the organisational aim of your setting. Secondly, you need to be clear as to what it is you are trying to make a decision on. This might sound a bit obvious, but these two parameters will give you a 'bottom line' where no others exist.

## 2. Collect information

What do you need to know in order to make the decision? You may already feel that you have many facts relevant to your decision in your head, but just to be on the safe side, put them down on paper. This not only means that you can easily check facts when making a decision, but also means that you will be able to feel more confident about having considered the facts. If you need more information, you may need to do some research into the topic, and you will need to build in extra time for this.

## 3. Identify options

Most decisions will have several possible outcomes. Make a list of all the outcomes that you can think of and then try to come up with a couple more that you wouldn't normally have thought of. Remember that at this stage you are not making a judgement on the options – just write them all down and see what they look like for now.

## 4. Consider the options and make the decision

One of the best ways to weigh up the options is to set each one against the organisational aim and objectives of the setting. Which option seems to fit more closely with what the service is trying to achieve? Some may immediately appear to go against your aim and can be thrown out straightaway. Others may need a bit more careful consideration and you may have to include judgements about other factors such as resources, legislation and so on in order to reject some of the rest.

## 5. Make contingency plans

Not wishing to be overly pessimistic about these things, but it is always possible that the decision you made will not turn out to be the one that you would have made with the advantage of hindsight. If it does all go wrong as a result of your decision, it is best to have done some thinking beforehand about how you would handle this situation. It is often the case that decisions need to be made with insufficient information and so it is important to try to anticipate possible outcomes and to consider what you will do about them if they happen.

The simplest and often most effective way of drawing up contingency plans is to list all the things that could go wrong, and against each one write what you would do about it. Then put the list away and forget about it. At least if you do need to manage yourself, your team and your organisation out of a crisis you will have already thought about how to get started and will feel more in control of the situation as a result.

## 6. Implement the decision

Introduce the decision and put it into place. You will find more on how to do this in Chapter 6.

## 7. Monitor and evaluate the decision

Decide how long you will monitor for – in other words, how long you will give the decision time to settle down – and then evaluate the decision in the light of the impact on your setting. (You will find more information on how to do this in Chapter 10.) You can also use reflective practice to help you to evaluate your own part in the decision-making process.

---

# Case study (Part 2)

Conrad puts an afternoon aside to make his decision. He gets out the mission statement of the playbus, which states that the playbus 'aims to provide play opportunities in communities where little or no play provision already exists'. He also reminds himself that he has to make a decision about whether to change the way that the sessions are run to incorporate literacy support.

Conrad collects information from the external bodies on what literacy support would involve. He researches the value of free play in children's development by reading some books and doing some research on the web. He also finds the results from the children's evaluation of the last summer project.

He then lists his options that he had identified earlier and wonders if he could come up with any more. He adds the following to his list:

- Ask for funding for specialist workers to come on board and run literacy support for those that want it in parallel with the free play sessions

- Make a presentation to the funders on the value of what we are planning to do and suggest other ways of providing literacy support.

Conrad looks at his list of options and decides that the last one best fits with what the playbus was set up to do. It would also give the playbus a chance to make a more general point about the value of its work. Conrad decides that, in case the external bodies were not convinced enough, he should have the second-to-last option as his contingency plan. If they did have to incorporate an educational aspect, then it could be offered on the basis of choice so that children wouldn't have to miss out on their play opportunities.

Conrad put his decision into practice by putting a lot of work into his presentation and he asked his team to help him with ideas about what it should contain. Following his presentation he monitors his decision to make the presentation by gauging the response of those present. He does this by asking them whether they feel that making the presentation had been a good idea. He made his evaluation of whether he has made a good decision based on the results of his monitoring.

# Developing your own skills

## Accepting responsibility

Managers do have to make decisions and be responsible for the decisions they make. Managers who do not accept full responsibility for making decisions are in danger of something called 'paralysis by analysis'. In other words, they are so worried by the fact that they might not make the best decision that they are unable to make any decision whatsoever. It is true that some decisions will not work out as you would have hoped, but in previous chapters we have looked at the need to accept imperfection, and this is also true of making decisions. The important thing is to accept that a bad decision, as long as it was made properly in the first place, appeared to be the best decision at the time that it was made.

Compromise is a fine technique with which to deal with many situations, but when it comes to making management decisions, it can only be the manager who is responsible for this. Managers should not be tempted to make decisions that are designed to keep two sides of any debate happy. This course of action is not a decision, it is a compromise, and it is important that managers do not mix up the two. After all, it is the manager who is going to be held accountable for any decision that is taken and so the manager needs to make sure that they have taken a particular line of action for the best reasons.

Of course it is often a good idea to involve others in making decisions. Some positive reasons for involving others are:

- other team members have different knowledge and experience;
- team members can feel that being involved in decisions makes them more part of the setting – they feel more included;
- team members who have played a part in making a decision which they support will work harder to make it succeed.

However, if managers choose to involve others in making decisions they must be clear (both with themselves and with others) that they are asking for ideas and views. Managers should not ask team members to make the decisions for them.

Some decisions that managers make will prove to be unpopular. Managers may find themselves being challenged about their decisions, either directly or indirectly. Managers need to be confident enough to explain their decisions logically and clearly and to stand by the decisions they have made. If the decision turns out to be less than perfect, managers need to accept responsibility for the decision and to be honest with others about how they would make the decision differently next time.

## Professional integrity

Any decision must first and foremost be in line with the organisational aim of the setting and be taken in the light of what the setting wants to achieve. In any organisation it is inevitable that personalities will come into play and sometimes obscure the decision that needs to be made. It is the job of the manager to listen to views and ideas, where they consider it

## First person – taking responsibility

I noticed that the team were regularly stopping children doing anything that involved the slightest amount of risk. I talked to some people from another after-school club and realised that things didn't have to be that way – although it was going to be a big decision to encourage the staff to let children do more risky things! First of all I decided that we weren't talking about 'anything goes' – the children still had to be 'safe enough' in our after-school club! I found out lots of information – about risk assessment, about why risk is important for kids, about the reality of us getting sued...I also did some observations in the club and made a list of things we could let children do, instead of stopping them. All this information seemed to be telling me that the children could easily cope with more risk, so I decided to talk about what I had found out at the next meeting.

After-school club Leader

appropriate, and then to steer a clear course through all of those contributions to decide what will best meet the aim of the setting.

Effective managers do not make decisions based on what is good for individuals – they make decisions based on what's best for their setting (even when there are people involved in, or affected by, the decision being taken). Managers in child-centred settings need to be aware that, even when decisions affect or involve people they may be friendly with at work, their job is to make decisions for the good of the children in their setting.

### Intuition

John Adair (2011) talks about 'sensing' the effects of the decision as an important part of evaluation. In other words, what does the setting feel like once the decision has been implemented – how do people seem to be coping with the change? Intuition, or 'gut feeling', can play an important part in decision-making, and managers can take into consideration their intuition when making decisions as well as when evaluating them.

It is important to listen to gut feelings, but not to rely on them to tell you what decision to make on their own. It is also important to remember that it is very difficult to tap into intuition if you are too tired, stressed or worried. The more pressured you feel, the less intuition will be available to you.

## Putting it into practice

- Managers do not have to make all the decisions in the setting, even if they are ultimately responsible for them.

- Make a decision about which day-to-day practice decisions you need to take and which you can pass on to others.

- All decisions should be taken in line with what is best for your setting and ultimately for the children you work with.
- Use the seven step process to help you to develop a clear and logical decision-making process for operational and development decisions.
- Use intuition as part of your decision-making process.
- Remember that making a decision is not the same as reaching a compromise.
- Accept that not all decisions will turn out according to plan and develop contingency plans even when you think they will.
- Be prepared for some of your decisions to be challenged or to be unpopular.
- Use reflective practice to learn from past decisions and to develop your decision-making skills.

# Giving feedback

A major part of the manager's role is to give feedback to individuals and the team as a whole. How else will people know whether the job they are doing is of the standard required and meets the objectives of the setting?

However, feedback is often misconstrued as the manager's chance to say what they want and to use it as an opportunity to inform individual team members about what they are doing wrong. Effective management processes include times when feedback is given that is neither of these things. Nor is feedback a formal evaluation – that is covered in Chapter 10. Feedback is the process by which a manager states their aims and objectives, opinions and ideas on a given topic/idea/suggestion/action/task to a team member to assist that individual in their work and to make clear the overall aims of the setting. A manager has the right to inform people of changes that need to take place and the team has the right to be informed. An effective feedback process allows this to happen.

## Essential skills for giving feedback

- Understanding the different methods of giving feedback
- Preparing and planning
- Understanding expectations
- Being aware of the basic 'dos' and classic 'don'ts' when giving feedback
- Giving objective criticism
- Giving praise
- Receiving feedback.

## Why is feedback important?

It is a manager's job to make sure that the team is doing what they are supposed to be doing according to their job description and required duties. After all, if you don't, who will? Managers who offer regular feedback opportunities are creating an atmosphere where concerns, ideas and suggestions can be heard and used to make improvements. It is also an opportunity to explain a process, a working practice or procedure and to explore individual ways of working with the idea. Feedback can also offer a chance to praise good practice and stop poor practice and to deal with potential issues before they develop.

Giving effective feedback requires the manager to plan and prepare carefully so that team members do not end up feeling humiliated or put down. There are a range of skills that a manager can develop to do this.

## Developing your own skills

There are a number of ways of offering feedback to a team and managers can use several methods alongside one another. It is important to decide which is most appropriate for the person and for the type of feedback to be given.

### Method one

Regular supervision sessions with individual team members.

### Method two

Regular team meetings with agenda items on tasks and responsibilities that allow feedback from everyone.

### Method three

Review meetings which have a set purpose of reviewing how specific projects or ideas are progressing.

### Method four

Annual or biannual appraisal sessions with a formalised process of logging feedback which each party prepares beforehand, followed up by discussions during the meeting on targets, responsibilities, training needs, and any issues of concern.

### Method five

Informal discussions where the manager can give and receive feedback as part of the normal working day.

## Choosing a method

The method chosen will depend on what the team and/or individuals are working on. Project work, such as organising the repainting of the building, will require daily or weekly feedback for both the manager and the team.

Individual feedback is best given in one-to-one supervision (method one), which should happen regularly – at least once every month. Supervision sessions are about daily tasks and responsibilities and medium-term goals. In appraisal sessions (method four), more long-term goals are discussed and agreed. If a manager has to give objective criticism about an individual's performance, one-to-one supervision (method one) is the most effective, rather than catching people on the hop when their attention is focused on something else.

## First person – developing opportunities for feedback

I used to have an 'open door policy' where anybody could come and see me at any time to talk about anything they wanted to. I thought it was a good idea to make sure that people knew that I was approachable. But I realised that not only did it mean that I was constantly interrupted and never really got anything done, it also meant that I spent all my time dealing with everybody else's issues – I never really got the opportunity to suggest new ways of doing things or to introduce better practice in some situations. Staff always talked to me, but I hardly ever got the chance to talk to them! So I gradually moved away from the 'open door' to setting up supervision sessions, which I can plan in advance so that I get the chance to give regular feedback to everybody instead of just dealing with what's in front of me.

Nursery Manager

If a manager wants to give the whole team feedback on their joint performance and/or practice, use method two or three. These methods allow for a group discussion and not only enable the manager to hear from the team as a whole, but also may allow the manager to make some important observations about how the group works together. These methods are also very useful for ensuring that everybody receives the same message at the same time, which may avoid misunderstandings or misinterpretations in the future.

## Case study

Latitia was showing a prospective parent around the nursery and witnessed a member of her team running story time with the use of a puppet and a drum. The children were enthralled with the story and joining in with the puppet on cue. When the parent had gone, Latitia made a point of going back into the room to speak to the member of staff to give her feedback: 'The story session seemed to be going very well; I loved the use of the puppet and the drum to keep the children's attention. Well done!'

## Preparation and planning

In preparing for giving feedback, managers need to reflect on what they are trying to achieve by giving it in the first place. Telling someone off may give us power momentarily, relieve pent-up emotions for a little while and satisfy our egos, but ultimately it will not encourage that team member to change their practice or attitude. We need to develop confidence (see Chapter 1) to give effective feedback and to be aware of when we as managers are not being clear or honest.

Think about why you are giving the feedback, who the feedback is to, what the effects of the feedback could be and what you want from the process, and how best to deliver the feedback. A useful way of remembering this is:

## Subject, Receiver, Outcome, Method = SROM

In giving feedback that involves criticism of performance, a manager should create the opportunity for discussion and self-reflection. Giving any sort of feedback should be a **constructive** event, **not** a negative one.

## Preparing

- Write a list of no more than three key points – any more will be too much to take on and 'muddy' the thinking of the receiver.
- Make the points specific.
- Write down some examples to give in the feedback.
- Make a list of reasons or background information that support your criticism and/or praise – brief notes will do.
- Think about the receiver: how are they going to 'hear' what you are saying? Are they uncomfortable receiving praise or criticism? How can you make it easier?
- If giving critical feedback, think of some positive things the team member has also done.
- Do not attack the person; comment on their actions and behaviour.

## Planning

- Think about the best time of day to give feedback.
- Think about where the feedback will take place – some managers do not have a separate office in which to hold meetings and so a private, quiet place somewhere else will be needed if having a one-to-one discussion.
- If you believe it may be a difficult session, have some water or tea/coffee ready. Allow more time, and do not plan it for the end of the day, as the person will go home without having time to assimilate what you have said and, possibly, sound other colleagues out.

## Case study

Latitia, as deputy manager of a large nursery, had to give feedback to Eileen, who was not answering the door or the phone to parents in a courteous or friendly manner. This had been raised in a general discussion during a team meeting where she had hoped that Eileen would pick up on this. Latitia planned to raise the matter during a supervision session and used the SROM acronym above to help her plan the meeting.

She knew the Subject was about working with parents and how the nursery was perceived by them; she knew that Eileen was good with the children, friendly and helpful with other colleagues but not always mindful of her own way of communicating. She anticipated that Eileen (Receiver) would be embarrassed and probably defensive when she mentioned this, so she thought the Outcome had to be that she would be made aware and shown what is expected of her so she could practice it. Latitia felt that the best way of using this (Method) was to sandwich what she had to say between some praise of Eileen's recent work with the children and then to ask Eileen her own thoughts on the work with parents, e.g. 'Where do you think you could make an impact?' Latitia wrote some questions down that she would ask Eileen, as well as the points that she wanted to make.

## Understanding expectations

It's important for managers to remember that in high pressure environments (and in our experience most settings fall into this category!), individual expectations about how tasks, issues, situations are dealt with which are not in line with the setting's vision or procedures can lead teams into dysfunctional ways of working.

Looking at the case study, there are several possibilities to explain Eileen's behaviour and attitude. She may, for example, believe that dealing with parents is not her job or her responsibility – her expectation may be that the manager always deals with parents. The manager's expectation, however, may be that all staff deal with parents as and when required, and always do so courteously and professionally.

## Giving praise

Acknowledgement is important. Humans learn as much from success as from mistakes. By offering thanks, approval, commendation, managers are supporting the individual, acknowledging their good practice and raising their confidence, thus benefiting the individual and the setting. Managers who reflect on their own experiences can see when someone saying 'thank you' has given them self-worth and a sense of satisfaction. The opposite is also true: when managers have experienced not being thanked for the work they have done, feelings of being taken for granted can grow, motivation is reduced, and work can suffer. On the other hand, heaping huge amounts of praise onto someone can sound insincere and they will not respect the next feedback or take the manager seriously.

Do not be put off giving positive feedback by someone brushing off what you say; it is largely due to embarrassment and false beliefs. However, if you know someone is very uneasy about being thanked, take them to one side instead of offering it in a group setting, but acknowledge the work briefly in the team meeting, e.g. 'Hafiz's work on the mural outside has really brightened up the place, don't you agree?' Deliver praise in a manner you know will be understood.

Think about who the praise is for, keep it sincere, give examples of what was good or successful and do not 'waffle'. By making the praise specific, a manager is giving information to the receiver about what is good so that they can repeat it. In addition do not sound apologetic: saying something like, 'I hope you do not mind me saying…' can make you sound insincere. Avoid also putting yourself down as a way of giving positive feedback: for example, 'If only I had your skills…' can be misconstrued as sarcasm.

## Giving objective criticism

At some stage a manager will have to pass on information to a member of a team that is not going to be easily received. Managers who avoid dealing with the issue of poor performance/ bad practice will face conflict at some stage. Criticism can be received negatively if the ground is not prepared first – remember that the goal of delivering objective criticism is to change performance or attitudes. Objective criticism is aimed at the actions, attitude or behaviour, not at the person. For example, 'May Chi, you are always laid back; is that why you are late?' attacks the person and then says what the behaviour is, rather than solely focussing on the behaviour that needs to change. Describing as clearly as possible what the manager is not happy with or what the complaint is about will help the team member see what it is that they are being asked to change. Expressing criticisms objectively by using facts, helps to ensure feedback is not taken as a personal attack.

By telling them how they have affected the general work of the team, and/or their own responsibilities, the manager can show how an individual's actions play a major part in team dynamics. Managers should not presume that the individual has remembered a previously agreed point, or that the individual is solely to blame.

## Why people do not 'hear' criticisms

There are a number of ways that individuals react to receiving criticism of their work. Here are a few:

- they take it personally – 'I am always being got at';
- they flatly deny they had anything to do with the concerns being raised;
- they blame others – 'my husband's car, it broke down and then the bus was late';
- they do not hear fully what you are saying because they only have negative experiences of feedback.

Some pointers to help with the above four reactions when giving negative feedback:

1.  By introducing the issues without too many details, a manager can ease the situation for the receiver; after all, they may not have any idea of what they have done that is not acceptable or why they are about to receive criticism of their work. By giving brief and clear reasons for raising the issues of concern a manager can support their points of criticism and it will not be seen as a personality clash/personal dislike, etc.
2.  It is important that there is agreement on the criticisms raised (remember, no more than three points). By asking 'open' questions a manager can check that the person has agreed with the issues raised, and giving time for the other person to respond allows the manager the chance to hear information that may be new to them. In cases where this happens the manager must modify the criticism and if necessary withdraw it. (An open question is one where you get more than yes/no in reply, e.g. 'Can you tell me how you feel the activity went?').
3.  A manager should always ask the individual if they have any ideas for resolving the situation. Owning the solution can help the individual not only accept the criticism, but also feel they can improve their behaviour. It will also bring up any difficulties that they may be experiencing that impact on their performance and have resulted in the type of feedback now being given.
4.  The final stage is summarising the agreed action to be implemented by the team member and placing a time limitation on when this will be achieved by.

In addition to the points above, use steps in 'dos' and 'don'ts' to guide you through preparing and giving criticism of team performance. Always think before acting, diagnose the situation first, and remember the person's previous performance and competence before launching in with criticisms.

## First person – giving focused feedback

One of my centre leaders phoned in a couple of hours before she was supposed to be at work to say that she couldn't come in that day as she only had two bras and they were both in the wash. As a bloke I didn't quite know what to do with that information, so I just said thanks for letting us know and put the phone down! After I'd calmed down a bit I knew I had to talk to her about this, but also knew that it had to be planned properly or I would end up getting into all sorts of inappropriate conversations. So I made some notes about how she was running a really good centre, but if she let us down at the last minute then it causes all sorts of problems for children and staff. The next day I went down to her centre and whenever it sounded like the conversation was going to stray into unwanted territory, I just kept repeating my basic point until she said that she understood how important it was not to let us down again.

Play service Manager

# Feedback 'dos' and 'don'ts'

Here are some straightforward 'dos' and 'don'ts' when giving feedback:

## DO

- sit in as relaxed a manner as you can and sit opposite the other person, if possible
- maintain eye contact
- use 'I' statements such as 'I liked', 'I have noticed'
- keep the tone matter-of-fact
- introduce the topic in an appropriate way: 'I wanted to…', 'I feel we ought to discuss…'
- keep it factual – point out exactly what it is you are happy with/not happy with
- give reasons/background briefly
- ask for suggestions or solutions if giving criticism of practice
- be firm if the action/behaviour has been repeated
- get a response by asking, 'Do you realise…?' 'Have you noticed…?'
- summarise – 'So let's agree that you will…'
- keep notes on the meeting, write them up and give a copy to the team member/s to check and agree; keep a copy of their agreement on file
- be fair.

## DON'T

- rush the session/feedback (even if you are nervous!)
- attack the person, e.g. 'You're lazy'
- use a negative tone or body language
- be put off by the other person's aggressive body language and/or tone
- be put off by silence. Ask open questions, offer a beginning of an answer to help them if they are truly stuck
- do other things at the same time
- be insincere in your praise
- threaten: instead use organisational policies to point out procedures
- use phrases such as, 'It's your own fault'
- hide behind your organisation or other people, e.g. 'The management committee think they know everything and want me to get you to…'

# Receiving feedback

It is just as important for a manager to receive feedback as it is to give it. An effective manager will want to hear what their team feel and think about the work they do and the way that they are being managed. It also builds good relationships within the setting by allowing issues and ideas to be aired. Make room at team meetings to hear what the team have to say and ask them for ideas or suggestions over plans or actions that you may have to take. Structure the supervision sessions so team members know they can have their say.

A manager's own experience will have an impact on how they receive feedback from the team. Some hints for receiving criticism are given here:

- If you are unclear what the criticism is about, ask for clarification and for an example. Avoid aggression such as 'You haven't got an example, have you?'; try saying it another way: 'I would find it helpful if you could give me some examples of that'.

- If criticism is given aggressively in the form of a personal attack, do not respond likewise. Instead, separate, if possible, what the criticism is about from the personal references. It may be necessary to point out to the other person that their approach has been very personal and you feel attacked.

- If you do not agree with the criticism, say so. However, do not do this aggressively and dismiss what the other person is saying altogether; rather encourage dialogue: 'So what you are saying is…'

- Look at the broader picture: are there issues not being mentioned here that are the root cause of the criticism? For example, have you not done something that you had agreed to do?

- As in the process of giving effective feedback, summarise with the person and suggest some action points you both can agree on. Use 'I' statements throughout to keep this objective.

# Putting it into practice

- Spend time thinking about when you want to give feedback and what the best method of doing so is.

- Develop your own confidence in giving feedback by practising doing it.

- Plan and prepare before you give feedback – remember SROM…

- Remember to find something to mention that's positive before giving the negative and always finish on a positive.

- Check personal feelings and thoughts – 'Am I doing this for me?'

- Practice the things you want to say by writing them down in different ways, then choose the best way for the individual/s you are giving feedback to.

- Be aware of the defence systems we use; ask the individual if they have understood or agree with what you have said.

- Be open to others' feedback on you; this may be useful to you developing your own skills and experience.

- Always write down feedback that you may need to refer to it another time.

- Remember you as a manager have the right and the duty to give feedback to the team to get the job done.

# Change management

The term 'change management' refers to a carefully planned process of making changes to either a part or all of the way an organisation operates. Change should always occur within an organisation in order to achieve something which will help to achieve the organisational goal. The change process is usually developed and led by a manager in the organisation, and it takes place over a period of time which will vary according to what sort of changes are being made.

It could be argued that managers in child-centred settings have an even harder task than most other managers when it comes to making changes. In a field which has traditionally been seen as a people-centred, caring profession, it can be hard for managers to make changes when they know that their team members and others may be personally affected – and not always for the better. We can all no doubt think of a time when we have been affected by change and probably can remember thinking that the change should have been made either faster or slower, or perhaps with more communication. Change management is one of the hardest parts of any manager's role, as ensuring that change happens (and happens successfully) requires managers to invest a great deal of time and energy in the process.

## Essential skills for managing change

- Confidence
- Vision
- Analytical thinking
- Planning
- Understanding individual responses to change
- Time management
- Leadership
- Giving feedback
- Monitoring and evaluation.

# Why is it important to manage change?

There are, of course, ways of making change happen in organisations that do not involve managing the process. Many managers, perhaps those who do not feel comfortable themselves with change or confident in their abilities to effect change, will simply tell their teams that a change has been put into place and leave the team to get on with it. While change management may look and feel like a long-drawn-out process, managers in child-centred settings can use it to help their team feel supported and valued through the process. The additional benefit will be that the change is more likely to happen and improvements to the service will be made. Managing change can also help you to ensure that not too many changes are being made at one time, as this can be detrimental to achieving progress.

Managing change needs to be approached like any other sort of project, with careful planning, a clear programme of events that need to happen, the involvement of others and more time than you probably originally thought it would take. Change cannot and will not happen overnight, and if you try to force change without treating the process like a separate piece of work, it may not happen at all. The other possible outcome of not managing change is that you will not achieve what you planned to achieve, and this could result in unhappy and disappointed team members. It is also possible that things will happen during, or as a result of, the change that you had not envisaged. Like any other project, contingency plans need to be put into place well in advance.

Another issue for managers to take into account when planning change is that to make changes within an organisation often means that you need to attempt to change the people within it. Changing their work practice requires them to examine and change their ideas, their values, their beliefs, and sometimes even their worldview. They may have to revise long-held and cherished ideas and attitudes and they may have to move out of their 'comfort zone' in order to begin new ways of working. None of this is easy for anybody to do in any circumstances. In a work situation where change is not an option, individuals can sometimes feel a huge amount of pressure to change in a relatively short space of time. This can cause stress for the individual and disruption in the setting, especially if an individual cannot see the point of the changes that have been planned. A carefully managed change process can take account of the time and support people will need to change, and is therefore likely to get more effective results than change which is simply dropped on people.

## First person – supporting change

I'd been promoted from room leader to deputy manager. Unfortunately this just meant that I was trying to do two jobs instead of one, as my old room colleagues were not as pleased about my promotion as I was and still relied on me doing a lot of the things I used to do for them. So eventually I made a list of all the things that I needed to do in my new job, and all the things that I used to do in my old one. I went to the next room meeting and gave everybody a copy of both lists, explained what my new role was and said that we needed to make sure that all the jobs on the room list were covered by people who worked there. I helped the staff to discuss how this was going to happen and they all agreed who was going to take on which jobs.

Nursery Deputy Manager

It is important to be aware that most types of change will involve extra resources of some description. Managing a change process will enable you to make plans for additional resources and to think about how you will provide these. Types of extra resources you and your team might need (both during the change process and also possibly once the change has taken place) include:

- Time
- Money
- Staff cover
- Equipment
- Outside support or expertise (for example, building advice, legal help).

Finally, it is worth repeating that change should always happen in line with what the organisational aim sets out to achieve. Sometimes it is easy to forget that the purpose of change is to develop the service provided by the organisation. Change should never be introduced because a manager is bored or feels that changing things will help them to assert themselves in the setting. Ensuring that there is a clear link between the proposed change and the development of the setting will mean that change is more likely to be successful.

# Internal and external influences

There are two types of factors which cause change in child-centred settings – internal influences and external influences.

Internal influences could include:

- children requesting changes in the way things are done;
- team members identifying that a change in practice is needed;
- budgetary or funding issues (i.e. too much or not enough money);
- parents suggesting changes;
- management identifying areas where things should be done differently;
- expanding or shrinking the service.

External influences may include:

- legislation changes;
- requirements to comply with a quality assurance scheme;
- OFSTED or other inspectors identify areas for change;
- technology being updated;
- competition – e.g. a new nursery opens down the road, a local authority subsidised after-school club offers cheaper sessions, etc.;
- funding bodies changing how they operate and what they will give money for.

To some extent, internal influences can be managed more easily. Managers can usually be more in control of deadlines and can therefore decide on the appropriate timescale in which to make the change. With external influences there is often more pressure to make the changes in a pre-determined length of time (because, for example, the Health and Safety Officer is coming back in three weeks' time, or because a piece of legislation has already come into force). Both types of change require careful planning, although managers need to recognise that external influences can lead to more stress and worry, both for themselves and the rest of the team.

## Four-stage model of change management

Managers and everybody else involved in a change process need to be very clear about what that process will involve. There is a simple four-stage model which can be useful in helping to plan and to keep track of the progress of change:

- Analysis
- Planning
- Implementation
- Monitoring and evaluation.

We will discuss analysis and planning in more depth in the section on 'developing your own skills' later on in this chapter.

Implementation of the plan should start on the planned start date and by then everybody should have been informed individually as well as in groups and individual concerns should have been addressed. By the start of the plan everybody should also be aware of their new roles and competent to take them on.

The change process can be monitored and evaluated in several ways. These could include:

- how effective the plan was;
- how much impact the change has made;
- whether the aim of the plan has been achieved;
- how people involved in the process feel about the change.

Monitoring and evaluation could be done on more than one occasion, depending on the length of the change process – for example, you may want to monitor how people feel about the change just before it happens, while it's happening, just after it has happened and six months after it's happened.

There is a final stage to the process which you may like to add if things go according to plan – and that is celebration! As we've already said, many people find change hard, and some sort of acknowledgement or even reward during and after the change process will not only be a great motivator but will also show team members that their efforts have been appreciated.

# Developing your own skills

## Analytical thinking

By analytical thinking we mean the need to be able to think about an issue in a rational, logical way. This type of thinking also involves some sort of detachment from whatever it is that you need to think about, which means being able to step back and consider the issue objectively. This can be quite hard to do, because we all have our own personal biases in the way that we see things at work. In child-centred settings it is common for managers to have made some sort of emotional investment in the way things have been set up or the way things work, and this emotional investment can naturally cloud our judgement as to what the true picture is. A useful skill therefore, analytical thinking helps us to make decisions and judgements with as much unbiased information to hand as possible.

Before beginning to plan the way things are going to change, managers need to understand the way things are in their setting now. This may sound a little odd, because everybody takes it for granted that they know how their setting works. However, what's needed at the start of any change management process is an objective view of what goes on in your setting. Here are some questions that you might find helpful to think about.

## What is acceptable and what isn't?

By this we don't mean what do your policies say, but how do things get treated in practice? What, for example, is the general attitude to turning up late for work? How creative are people when it comes to solving problems – or do they always come to you for the answers? Do people turn a blind eye to personal phone calls? Is babysitting for parents allowed and, if it isn't, does it go on anyway?

## What spoken and unspoken rules exist?

For example, is it assumed that if a parent is late then somebody will stay with the child (rather than putting their coat on and leaving you with the child every time)? Does everybody always go on social outings and, if people don't go, do they get left out of general discussions during work time? Is there a hierarchy – June always collects the fees because she is most senior, for example (even though in practice there is no reason why any of the team members can't collect the fees)? Is it 'accepted practice' that Dave is the 'craft expert' and nobody else does craft with the children?

By asking these types of questions and looking objectively at the answers you should begin to draw up a picture of your setting and your team in terms of how receptive to change they are.

Management theory suggests that you are more likely to succeed in bringing about effective change if the culture of the organisation can be preserved. For example, if your analysis tells you that your setting is used to routine and it doesn't rely on people being creative to deliver the service, you need to bear this in mind when planning your change. If change involves putting into place something which is routine and predictable, you will have less resistance and therefore more chance of the change succeeding. If the change requires people to be more creative both during and after the change process, however, then you will have to allow extra time and support for this in your planning. If you are going to try to change the culture of the organisation, then you need to first ensure that people feel comfortable with the change before the change actually takes place – after all, you are about to move them out of their comfort zone.

## Planning

Managers need to draw up written plans for putting the change into effect and the plan should include:

- The goal you are aiming to achieve through the change process (see Chapter 2 for more on this).
- The timescale over which the change will take place and what will happen when – this needs to be very specific so you can monitor your progress, e.g. 15 May, team meeting. The timescale should also have a clear start and finish date.
- Who will be involved in the change and how they will be consulted and involved in the process.
- The resources you already have and additional resources you will need.
- Any budgetary/financial implications.
- Who will be involved in leading and managing the change and what their roles will be in the process – it is sometimes possible for people in the team to be involved in supporting you and for them to take on some of the work.
- The key stages involved in the timescale and what contingencies you will put into place if these have not been achieved.
- Communication details – who gets to know what when. This is crucial – not having a clear plan to disseminate information can lead to rumours and gossip which can hinder the change process.
- How the change will be monitored and evaluated.
- How achieving the change will be celebrated, both the small steps along the way and the whole project.

# Case study

Inspired by a training course, Sonia went back to her playcentre that evening and took a good hard look at the way that the setting was laid out. She thought about what she had learnt on the course and could see how to make the centre much more child-friendly. When everybody had gone home, Sonia stayed behind for several hours until late at night, moving furniture, throwing out broken toys, changing notice boards and completely revamping the whole setting so that it looked completely different.

Pleased with the results, Sonia eagerly looked forward to her team's arrival and appreciation the next day when they came in to set up. However, she was very disappointed and quite cross at the reaction of the team. John arrived, made no comment about everything being in a different place but did swear on several occasions when he couldn't find anything. Amel arrived and didn't say anything about the changes. She just kept wandering around, not doing anything, as if she didn't know where she was anymore. Doug got to work and commented to the other two that some people obviously didn't have enough work to do if they had time to move furniture around.

When the children arrived they were surprised to see that things weren't where they had been yesterday. Some of them said that they liked the messy play better on the floor but Sonia did notice that the children were more disruptive than usual.

Sonia felt that all her hard work had been for nothing and her team were obviously not happy with her. The atmosphere in the centre was not good and the children picked up on this, which in turn caused more friction.

## Understanding individual responses to change

Not everybody has a negative reaction to change, but many people do, and the reasons for this are many and varied. Before embarking on any sort of change process, managers need to be aware of the reasons for individuals feeling negative about change and to develop strategies for combating the negativity. Reasons for dislike of change include:

- not understanding why change is necessary ('if it ain't broke, don't fix it');
- being too busy getting on with the job (this is particularly the case in child-centred settings where there are a whole lot of 'doers'!);
- the change involving a real or perceived threat;
- the individual having allegiances within the setting, which means that they are going to resist whatever you do, change included;
- fear of loss of control/insecurity about what the change will mean in the future;
- worries about increased workload;
- concerns about hidden agendas – 'This can't just be about changing the shift pattern; she must be trying to get rid of me';
- Uncertainty about their role during and after the change.

Managers need to identify the cause(s) of resistance to change in individuals, and then work out how to put to rest the fears and concerns for each person. When people are feeling worried and insecure, it is tempting for managers to 'beat around the bush' in an attempt to try to shield individuals from more aggravation. However, this course of action will generally cause more worry and insecurity, as the person concerned will sense that something isn't right and then think that there is more to the issue than there actually is. Managers need to be able to talk through the fact they think the person is unhappy about the proposed change, listen to any fears or concerns the individual might have and address those worries one by one (see Chapter 5).

Managers need to remember that dealing with change can be a very personal experience and that different people will need different levels of support at different times. People who are positive about change will also need support, as they will also be affected by change.

Managers are human beings too and will also have their own individual responses to change which they need to be aware of and deal with. It is advisable for managers involved in change management to get some support themselves, because when driving forward any kind of change it is important to stay focused and positive throughout. There may be times when it's hard and you feel like giving up, but it is vital to hold on to your vision and the fact that, if you don't lead the way, your setting will not develop in the way that you feel that it should.

## Leadership

When planning to make changes, it is essential to work out how you will take people with you. In a child-centred setting this could mean your team, your managers, the parents, the children, external bodies – some or all of these may be involved, depending on the sort of change you are making. In the case study above, Sonia was obviously excited about making changes and this was really positive. However, carried away by her enthusiasm, she forgot that as a manager her role was not to do the change herself, but to inspire and lead others in making the change together. Ways that managers can help people to feel more positive about change include:

- involving the individual in the change process, if they want to be involved;
- holding discussions about the need for change and asking for people's views on the proposed change;
- addressing individual fears and concerns;
- reminding them of the vision of a better service and going over the reasons for change;
- organising formal or informal training if the concerns are around lack of skills and/or knowledge;
- selling the change – point out not only the benefits for others but also the benefits for them.

# Case study

Sue, the manager of a small nursery chain, has been aware for some time that the separate settings do not work together. In fact, it seems to her that the managers in each setting did just about everything they can to work in isolation, rather than being part of the bigger team. When she visited some of the settings, she overheard negative conversations about the other sites, and there was apparently much jealousy and rivalry between the settings over things such as resources.

Sue knows that things have to change and wrote down what she would like to achieve: 'To ensure that all the nurseries work together in promoting a corporate identity in the next nine months.'

Over the next month she spent more time in each of the nurseries, listening and observing how things are done in each one. She learnt that each nursery had its own culture, but also that they all basically believed in the work that they were doing and wanted the best for the children in their care.

At the end of the month, Sue drew up her plan to implement change. She set the following objectives to help her to meet her aim:

- To arrange some training for staff from all the sites on the value of the work they were doing with the children. She felt that this would boost morale and help staff members to find common ground and see that they were all working towards the same thing. She would also organise a buffet lunch to make staff feel valued and attend the session herself, so that she could introduce the change to all of the staff at the same time.

- To review the budget for each setting and to share all the information with all the managers. She would involve the managers in the review so they could have an open discussion about whether resources were fairly allocated.

- To explain to the managers, prior to the training day, her vision for change on a one-to-one basis so that they could air any concerns. She recognised that the managers were key to selling her vision of a service which was coherent and cohesive.

- To arrange for all the managers to be trained together on corporate identity. She would ask them to bring what they had learned to a meeting to discuss how to take it forward.

- To arrange, in conjunction with the managers, job swaps for nursery nurses amongst the sites.

- To hold weekly management meetings to enable managers to keep her informed about how the job swaps, etc. were going. She hoped that by doing this she would encourage the managers to ask staff what they had learnt and how they had got on.

- To review all the policies, procedures and publicity and ask a group of staff made up from all the sites to work with her in order to standardise the documents. She felt that not only was this a good way of getting staff to work together but it would also mean that a clear picture should emerge of the similarities and differences between the sites.

Sue noted in her plans that there may be budgetary implications if she needed to close sites in order to get training done, but she decided that, as this wasn't a regular event and it was very important, it was all right to do this.

# Putting it into practice

- Making any sort of change in a setting needs to be carefully planned and managed.

- Be honest and realistic about where you are starting from and the pace at which you can reasonably expect change to take place.

- Remember that some people will welcome change and others will find it more difficult, so plans need to include ways of keeping everybody on board with the change.

- Address individual concerns and fears about change throughout the change process.

- Use the vision of the benefits the change will bring for the setting, the children and the team to help you to lead the team through the change.

- Make sure that your plan includes additional resources you will need, both during the change process and once the change has taken place.

- Keep everybody informed about progress and give positive feedback to individuals as well as to the group.

- Celebrate small successes during the change process as well as the final achievement of the whole project.

# Inclusive practice

The basic principles of inclusive management which underpin all the leader's work should be to value and involve each person with whom he or she works.

PIP Guidelines Series 1, 2002

Central to child-centred settings is the role of all workers to ensure equality of opportunity and implementation of anti-discriminatory procedures when providing a place for all children to play and learn. This means raising awareness, acknowledging differences, removing barriers but, more importantly, every adult working with children and young people learning to be a consistent, positive role model. When it comes to inclusive practice, a manager's role is to make sure that they and their team create an environment where children can reach their full potential without barriers which come from discriminatory attitudes and practices in the setting.

## Essential skills for inclusive practice

- Creating a climate of openness and tolerance
- Keeping up-to-date
- Raising awareness
- Positive interventions.

## Developing your own skills

Much of the manager's responsibilities with regard to inclusive practice will focus on monitoring behaviour, attitudes and procedures, plus supporting team members or children in understanding effective ways of responding to inappropriate remarks or behaviour. If part of your vision is to make your child-centred setting inclusive, how you and your team actively encourage positive relationships will be vital to realising this vision.

As we've already discussed in earlier chapters, the responsibility for making decisions and changes rests with the manager. So a manager's own understanding of how to be and what kind of role model they are in terms of inclusive practice supports the whole process for the team and the children.

## Creating a climate of openness and tolerance

It is not possible to know and understand everything about all the different cultures and heritages that make up the backgrounds of the children and young people of the British Isles or indeed even just those currently using your setting, so **ask.** It is better to encourage an atmosphere where people **enquire and do not assume**, where people are learning from each other and trying to understand, than develop prejudices on grounds of ignorance or develop avoidance reactions. By keeping up-to-date with information on the children using your setting and encouraging children and team members to be open-minded, you will be able to create a climate of openness and tolerance.

The role of a manager will include being open and frank with parents and children if what being asked is not possible and will go against policies of the service. For example, if a parent asks that their child does not eat certain foods for religious or health reasons, complying with this request is usually straightforward. On the other hand, if a parent asks that their daughter, aged 11, no longer be allowed to play on adventure playground equipment because it is not 'ladylike', that would be a request to question because it is discriminating against her on grounds of gender. Managers need to balance the rights of the child with respect for parents' wishes, and this sometimes means being honest with parents about the aims and policies of the setting.

> ## First person – supporting good practice
>
> Two of my team had come to have a 'quiet word' as they were concerned about something that kept happening at home time. One little boy was being picked up by his dad who was smacking him pretty much every day because the little boy wasn't quick enough getting his coat on. Although obviously upset by this, the members of staff said they didn't feel that they could intervene because the family were travellers and this way of dealing with children was 'their culture'. I had to remind them that it was our policy that there was no physical punishment on the play bus, regardless of the beliefs or backgrounds of the parents, and offered to talk to the dad next session.
>
> Playbus Leader

## Keeping up-to-date

A full understanding of inclusive practice will require a manager to know what 'equality' means both legally and in terms of best practice. Managers are of course responsible for the policies and procedures of the setting and this includes keeping them up-to-date and relevant to current practice. Any inclusion policy needs to say more than, 'we will not discriminate against a person because of their race, culture, disability, etc'. It will need to specify **how** the setting will not discriminate and **how** you are developing practices that are inclusive.

Reviewing policies and procedures and making sure that they are understood and being put into practice is an important way of keeping up-to-date. Team meetings or specially arranged discussions on the inclusion policy will allow views to be heard and questioned, and for everybody to deepen their understanding of what inclusion means in the setting. Discussing policies helps the team focus on what your setting believes and what is captured in your vision, and how this translates into practice.

Managers also need to keep up-to-date with current thinking on language and terminology, as this also changes all the time. Reading professional journals, researching on the internet and attending networking meetings and training courses can all help with this, and there are several suggestions for organisations and websites that can help with this in the back of this book.

## Raising awareness

It is important to raise awareness of the need for inclusive practice as not everybody has had the same experiences in working with children from a wide range of different backgrounds and abilities. Some members of staff may be less aware than others of how some of their beliefs and practices could stem from incorrect beliefs and assumptions (prejudices) about certain individuals or groups of people, and so it is important that managers make sure that they are promoting awareness of inclusive practice to combat stereotypical thinking in the setting.

Ways of raising awareness include:

- Having inclusion policies displayed for staff and parents to read.

- Reviewing the activities and resources offered to children (see Chapter 10). Think about whether certain activities encourage stereotyping, sexism or other barriers for some children and explore this with the team. This could be done verbally or by a questionnaire.

- Designing or buying in board games on inclusion and equality of opportunities to encourage discussions and learning appropriate to children's age of development.

- Choosing play materials, books etc which reflect the diversity of our society and encourage non-stereotypical thinking (for example, story books which include men as primary carers).

- Selecting non-stereotypical images for newsletters, brochures etc (for example, does your publicity always include pictures of boys playing football and girls making things?).

- Ensuring that comments and practices which may reflect stereotypical thinking are dealt with in a positive manner and encourage all team members to do the same.

Inclusion is just like any other part of our practice, in that it is constantly changing and moving on, so there will never be a 'perfect' inclusive setting. Managers need to create regular time to plan and reflect on raising awareness of current practice issues as managers will want to 'take the team with them' to keep inclusive practice up-to-date and relevant for the children they are currently working with (see Chapter 6).

# First person – developing awareness

My team really surprised me at our last team meeting as a couple of them asked why we were going through the inclusion policy because we were all white and all women – they also pointed out that we all had qualifications where we would have already 'done' inclusion. At least it opened up the subject for discussion, which was really useful as it brought up a couple of issues that clearly needed sorting out that I hadn't known about. It made me realise that we need to review our inclusive practice just like we would review the rest of our practice, as I can't take it for granted that my team all think and behave the same just because we work with children.

Nursery Manager

## Positive interventions

It is vital that all team members are aware of their role with regard to challenging discrimination and are given support in doing this. The team should have the opportunity to discuss a diverse range of methods for dealing with stereotypical thinking and discrimination that arises in the setting. This will not only help support them but also explore what attitudes prevail at the setting.

Managers need to develop the confidence to deal with any adult who makes a remark which goes against the inclusive nature of the setting. Holding an open discussion at a team meeting about adults' use of language can highlight the issue but is not always enough. In addition there may be a need to discuss on a private basis that team member's actions; this has the added benefit of helping them feel they have increased their understanding of discrimination rather than been picked on. Chapter 5 gives suggestions for how to deliver objective criticism which of course also applies to dealing with discriminatory behaviour or language, although the severity of the remark or behaviour would of course determine what action the manager would need to take.

## Case study

Tomás, manager of the after-school club, is sharing a table at snack time with Joseph, who is from East Africa and has not been in England very long. He notices that Joseph eats with his hands and not the knife and fork. One of the boys sitting at the table laughs at him and calls him a baby for not being able to use the cutlery. Tomás intervenes by asking the boy to stop laughing and explaining that people from different countries have other ways of eating. He then asks the boy who laughed what food he eats with his fingers, opening up the discussion to involve other things and then asks Joseph what he has found different.

Tomás challenged the behaviour of the boy that laughed and called Joseph a baby in a gentle way that involved all of them learning and understanding a little more about cultural differences and practices.

# Some 'dos' and 'don'ts' when responding to inappropriate remarks

## DON'T

- ignore any discriminatory remark even if it was 'meant' as a joke; it implies it is 'OK' here to say things like that;
- shout or get angry;
- threaten exclusion or sacking if the policies of the setting do not include this;
- fail to monitor and review because of lack of time or resources;
- give someone a book and tell them to read that instead of talking to them directly;
- only deal with it in private behind closed doors – this gives mixed messages to other team members.

## DO

- read up on policies and good practice;
- attend training or discussion groups on inclusive practice;
- bring up issues of dealing with discrimination in team meetings;
- have an open mind but be prepared to say 'that is not acceptable';
- look for ways that support team in good practice with regards to anti-discrimination, e.g. get a speaker or parent to discuss cultural issues at a team meeting;
- look at your own personal language and attitudes;
- review and monitor inclusion policies and make changes if necessary.

## Case study

Bella is one of the volunteers at a local playgroup. A mother brings her three-year-old child who has cerebral palsy. Bella says to the mother, 'I am afraid we have very little equipment for crippled children here.' Nur, the manager, hears this and comes over to the mother and Bella, saying to Bella, 'The child isn't a cripple, Bella; she has a physical impairment, that's all. We can adapt lots of equipment if we think about it'. Nur talks to Bella after the playgroup has finished; she asks Bella to sit down opposite her and explains to her that words and phrases can really cause offence, even if un-intentional. Nur asks Bella to reflect on her use of the word 'cripple' and points out why it is out of date and inappropriate. Bella is defensive and remarks that she has always used that word and grew up with it. Nur reminds her that the playgroup wishes to remain inclusive to all children and how important a resource it has been for local parents, and for that family in particular. Bella agrees to watch her language; in addition Nur mentions a few training courses that might help Bella to become more aware of up-to-date language.

# Putting it into practice

- Start by reflecting on your own approach and attitudes.

- Be aware of your own language and behaviour to watch out for hidden prejudices.

- Think about ways of acknowledging cultural diversity within the setting – even if you have no young people from other cultures.

- Discuss areas of potential discrimination in the setting at team meetings to improve skills and knowledge.

- Have clearly written policies on inclusion showing how the setting will both prevent and deal with discrimination.

- Have a mixture of equipment and books that all children, whatever their abilities, can access.

- Look into training some of the team in specific skills, e.g. learning sign language.

- Never leave discriminatory language or actions unchallenged.

- When dealing with intentional discrimination, remain calm but firm.

- Get advice and support from others to develop your setting's inclusive practice.

# Time management

Being able to plan work and programmes of activities is very important for managers in child-centred settings. Being able to plan and manage how we use our own time is just as important, but we do not always feel like this is in our control! Some people seem to be natural time-managers, whilst others need to develop the skills and master their own approaches to managing numerous tasks and responsibilities as a manager.

However, we all need to practise managing our time effectively, and the methods we use for doing this will change from task to task. Underlying these methods is our basic approach and attitude to time and time management, which can be developed with a few essential skills which can help us.

## Essential skills for time management

- Using methods to analyse how you use your time
- Saying 'no' and reinforcing personal boundaries
- Knowing your time wasters
- Knowing how to prioritise tasks
- Distinguishing between important and urgent tasks.

## Why is time management important?

This may appear obvious to some managers and not to others. We believe that by developing the skills to manage your time you will be a more effective manager, i.e. you will have increased confidence, less stress and more time to think. This in turn can make the job easier and more satisfying, with the spin-offs being increased enthusiasm for your role as a manager and time for more involvement with staff, volunteers, children and families.

Robert Heller and Tim Hindle (1998) suggest that the ideal allocation of time for managers should be as follows:

60 per cent of time on planning and development

25 per cent of time on projects

15 per cent of time on routine tasks.

In actual fact, for most of us is it very different, of course! It is more like:

60 per cent of time spent in routine tasks

25 per cent of time on projects

15 per cent of time on planning and development.

Many managers of child-centred settings are also part of the team working with the children, so would probably laugh at the idea of trying to reorganise their time to have 60 per cent of time on developing projects. However, by taking some time to look at our own working patterns, reorganising, planning or simply reinforcing boundaries and, of course, by being honest with ourselves, we may find we can get a little closer to the 'ideal' of 60 per cent than we had first thought.

There is no one method or set of rules that works better than another. We need to develop ways according to our priorities and the responsibilities of the job we are currently doing. For all methods your starting point is **your attitude** to time management. Do you want to change the way you are managing your time? Are you getting the job done the way you would ideally like to? How much time do you have to enjoy the work you do? Being aware of your own approach to time management, looking for ways that you can make improvements, is a useful exercise for all of us.

# Developing your own skills

## Tried and tested methods for analysing how you use your time

There are always demands that compete and on an average day time is 'wasted' by a series of tasks that get interrupted and not completed. In a child-centred setting much of the management of the setting is based around routines and helping the team and volunteers meet the needs of the children. It may be that a realistic analysis of your workload for your particular setting would show you need to spend a large percentage of your time on routine tasks. By analysing how we use our time we can see where we need to make adjustments and develop approaches that make best use of the time we have.

### Method one

Look at the various aspects of your role as manager of a child-centred setting; a job description, if you have one, will help with this. Make a list of daily tasks.

- Estimate how much time you spend on each of the tasks using half-hourly or hourly measurements. Add up the time spent on tasks. Is your total more than the hours you have in a day?

- Beside each of the tasks and time spent write what time you *would like* to spend on it. Add this up and compare it with the actual time spent.

- Write a list of things that frequently stand in the way of you achieving your plan for the day. This list of questions may help you:

  1. Am I doing anybody else's work?
  2. Am I doing something that a member of the team could do?
  3. Do some tasks take longer than I thought they would?
  4. Do I attend too many meetings?
  5. Am I saying 'yes' when I should say 'no'?
  6. Am I not making my needs clear?
  7. Have I allowed myself some thinking and planning time?
  8. Have I any patterns of work I am unhappy about?

- Using the breakdown of 'ideal' and 'actual' time used above, how would you break your day down? Are you spending more time on one group of tasks than you need to or would like to?

- Draw up a list of tasks that could be routine and must be done each day, a list of tasks that you would like to do and a list that could be delegated to another member of the team. Put this somewhere you can refer to it regularly during the day, such as a wall chart or on your computer desktop.

- Cross off tasks when you have done them – it makes you feel a lot better!

## Method two

- As for method one, call to mind all your tasks and write a list at random without thinking too much.

- Draw up a daily or weekly sheet with five main areas under these headings:

  Priorities Routine tasks Phone calls Meetings Carry forward

  Call it something such as My Daily/Weekly Action Plan or Tasks Sheet and track your action points over a period of time.

- Put items from your list in the relevant columns.

- By each item put a time period, e.g. 1.00–1.30 p.m. This way you can look to see if certain tasks are taking longer and ask yourself why. What you are looking for are areas you can change and habits that detract from completing tasks and hold you up from doing the planning and development side of your work (look at 'Knowing your time wasters' below to see if you recognise any in your work!).

When you know what distracts you and what takes up some of your time unnecessarily then you can start to build in 'defences' and alter your pattern of work and, therefore, become efficient in managing your time most of the day.

In addition to working on your own habits, think about what organisational habits have developed for others in the team; and how changing your own way of working could have an impact on theirs.

## First person – analysing time

I had always thought that, as we're a small nursery, I should do everything that the rest of my team does. I didn't want anybody to think that I was 'above them', so I made sure I did my share of the washing up, the cleaning, and everything else the rest of them did. It seemed totally unrealistic when I went on a course and was told not to clean the toilets because it wasn't my job! But after a few days back in the nursery I began to notice just how much of my job I wasn't doing. I was always busy doing stuff – but the things we'd talked about on the course just didn't get done. I never seemed to get a chance to sort out a proper induction for new staff, or update our training records, and I realised a whole year had slipped past without any appraisals happening…so I bit the bullet and at the next staff meeting talked about all the things that I should have been doing as a manager to develop the nursery. I explained that I couldn't do all of the things I had previously been doing as well, and so I was going to try to take a step back from day-to-day practice and concentrate on the things I had got behind on. The girls were great about it and a couple of them even said that they would like supervision sessions with me but had always been afraid to ask because I seemed so stressed out! Since then I've been ticking the jobs off my list slowly but surely, and of course I do 'muck in' every once in a while – just to keep my hand in!

Nursery Manager

## Saying 'no' and reinforcing boundaries

An important part of managing your own workload is setting boundaries for others (unless of course there is an emergency). Managers who are constantly interrupted by their team for decisions or information will never feel that they can get any substantial task completed.

Saying 'no' does not mean you are an authoritarian manager who is not available to support the team and/or children. It does mean that you have the right to allocate certain working time to the management tasks that need your full attention. If you have allocated time in the week or day to tackle a task that requires you to concentrate and focus, it is best not to accept any phone calls, visitors or disturbances. A simple explanation to all the team that this is what you are going to do normally suffices, but occasionally you will have to be assertive and repeat what it is you need. State very clearly what it is you need; do not use phrases such as 'I am afraid that…'. After all, as the manager you will need time to work on issues for the centre. It will be difficult if you do not have an office area; try and form a screen around you with other equipment or, if in a school, ask to use another room.

Voicing your needs can be done in a variety of ways such as; putting up a jokey sign (one of us uses a sign which says, 'Quiet, genius at work'!), mentioning in supervision and team meetings that you are going to have to work on your own with no disturbances and saying when and for how long; closing your office door and diverting calls or putting the phone on voicemail; placing the phone outside your office so others can answer it. Asking the management committee to find the funds for staff cover whilst you work at home on a task may be another option.

A final point: do be mindful of members of your team whose perceptions of time are different to yours. Clear explanations with patient reminding from time to time will show by example how you wish to operate.

## Case study

Geraldine, as manager of a large crèche, wanted to work on a new funding application form that required plans for extending the staff and space. She talked about her ideas for this at a team meeting and said to all the staff that she needed time to prepare the application and, therefore, would be in the kitchen (as she did not have an office) from 10.30 to 12.30 p.m. on the following Monday. She then said she would require the team to take all calls or visitors' queries unless there was an emergency. She emphasised that she would not open the door to any knock or answer any query; she also explained what she believed was an emergency that she could be disturbed for. On the Monday she reminded all staff and put a notice on the door to the kitchen. She made sure that she spent the two hours fruitfully and reappeared at 12.30 p.m. as she had stated she would.

## Knowing your time wasters

The usual time wasters that affect managers of child-centred settings include:

- delays in traffic/public transport;
- phone calls upon arrival, such as parents who have forgotten to give information;
- non-delivery or purchasing of essential items, such as the food for snack time;
- chatting over coffee;
- the team wanting advice, feedback, decisions etc while the manager is doing something else;
- team members arriving late, so the manager does tasks;
- parents/carers visiting unexpectedly and wanting to talk about their child;
- someone forgetting to finish a task so manager does it;
- inessential meetings, such as treasurer wanting to check figures given already;
- meetings dragging on beyond the time allocated;
- cleaners not doing their job;

- long phone calls;
- broken or old equipment;
- no voicemail.

## How to prioritise tasks

Think about how you rate something as being a 'priority'. Is it, for instance, because your management committee has asked for it? Is it to do with your legal obligations? Is it to make life easier for others? Is there a deadline, as for funding applications? What does 'priority' really mean for you and your setting?

Ask yourself, when writing your list of routine tasks and priorities, how important they are; list them A, B, or C. 'A' tasks are ones that you should try and complete every day (or at least a few of them); 'B' tasks are the ones that you spend most of your time doing; and 'C' tasks are those that you can do perhaps at the end of the day, or maybe they can be delegated, again usually routine tasks.

Evaluate your priorities as you go through the day, moving them accordingly. Occasionally you will have a conflict of priorities with your team or management committee or have many more listed than you can actually deal with. The following list may help if you find yourself in that situation:

- Try to do at least one of your 'absolutely essential' tasks each day and at least two of the tasks that need to be done, in addition to any routine tasks.

- If one of the tasks is boring, complicated, or generally not easy to do, tackle it *first thing* in the morning. It will make the day go better and give you a clearer mind to get on with other planned action points (this really works!).

- Allocate a time in the day when you will deal with all mail, phone calls and/or visitors; if need be, make this a quiet time and shut your door.

- If some priority tasks cannot yet be done because you are waiting for information or further details, put a note to yourself in a diary or on an action plan to chase it up so you can meet your deadline. If others need to know this, inform them as soon as possible.

- When thinking about a long-term plan and the term/year ahead, remember what cycles your work has; e.g. if your playgroup or after-school club closes during the holidays, your list of long-term action points will need to take this into consideration. Those that are a priority will have to be completed in the time cycle that you work in. Towards the end of a school term the team are generally tired and not able to muster a huge amount of enthusiasm for changes; bear that in mind when planning workloads.

- Remember to explain to others you are working with why a task may not be completed in time.

Remember also that priorities may change from day to day because of new information, emergencies that need to be dealt with and other events.

There is a different very easy and quick way of prioritising tasks which is simply this: If a task, or series of tasks, will only take three minutes each, by opting to do them all first you clear a lot of work. You can then use the rest of the time to prioritise what's left and/or tackle larger pieces of work without getting distracted by the smaller things.

## Case study

Frankie manages an adventure playground; she has a list of daily routine tasks. In addition, she has been working on her Level 3 in Playwork qualification and she has two units to finish by the end of the month to meet the deadline. There was an emergency yesterday, one of the team is off on First Aid training this week and Frankie will need to deal with two young people accused of bullying if they come to the centre today. Frankie draws up a list of all her tasks for this afternoon and what else she needs to do during the week. Her qualification work is important and she decides to prioritise that for the afternoon. Next she puts the emergency from yesterday at the top of her list, as she can write the report and letters within 30 minutes. She then decides to delegate dealing with the two accused of bullying to the senior playworker. She makes a note to talk to him as soon as he comes in and immediately gets out the file. She also makes a note to herself about dealing with bullying and accusations of this for the following week's team meeting, which reminds her she has not typed up the notes from the previous one yet. She then looks again at her list, puts a time by everything and decides to do the minutes first, then the qualification work, as the minutes will be useful evidence for her qualification, then she will do all routine tasks that take longer than three minutes.

This way Frankie goes through her list – not ignoring the routine tasks but reorganising what she has to do first, then second, and so on. She can delegate a task and this frees up her time. She now has a clearer idea of what she can get completed in the time she has.

## Urgent or important?

Tasks listed in your daily/weekly plan can be arranged according to their urgency or importance. Urgent tasks are those that need your attention or can be delegated straight away to be carried out within an immediate time frame. They will have major impact on the setting in some way, such as getting food supplies in for snack time. Important tasks are those that either need action but not straight away, or need several different points to be completed at different stages, e.g. ordering new stock or equipment before the end of term or before the summer playscheme begins. Being able to differentiate between the two will help you schedule your action plan accordingly and, of course, re-prioritise your list of tasks when necessary.

## Putting it into practice

● Planning your day and your week is *never* a waste of time. MAKE time to do it.

- Dealing with a difficult task, or part of it, straight away makes you feel better and leaves you thinking more clearly.

- Keep a diary or calendar with meetings, appointments, etc., visible.

- Every so often, monitor time needed for completing tasks against your plan.

- Ask more about meetings you are being asked to attend: Do you really need to go? Can a phone call or email do it instead?

- Ask parents to make an appointment to see you, unless they have an emergency.

- Allocate a time each day or each week that you can attend to tasks without interruptions.

- If you find you have too many 'absolutely essential' tasks then you will need to delegate some of your routine or 'better done today' tasks to others.

- Alter priorities when necessary – don't keep rigidly to your plan.

- Remember if you have set yourself a deadline it should be to help you, not to cause more stress. Give yourself a treat when you meet a deadline.

- Practice skills in time management, see where you can improve – don't give up!

# Building a team

There are two ways of looking at the manager's position when it comes to building the team. Some theorists would advise a manager to think of themselves as a team servant, being part of the team and not just managing it, balancing the roles of the individual staff members, the team as a whole and the task. Other theorists believe the manager is not part of the team but directing and supporting the team as a leader, leading from the front, monitoring aspects of the work, offering encouragement and vision, getting the job done. This theory also has many advantages, especially for child-centred settings, e.g. someone is always keeping an eye on the way ahead while the team are busy being with the children.

In addition to building and motivating the team, the manager may have a role as a referee dealing with team conflicts and clashes of personality. How you deal with this will depend on your own level of confidence and experience (see Chapter 1).

## Essential skills for team building

- Understanding of basic theory on how team traits and dynamics impact on teams
- Identifying individual and team strengths and weaknesses
- Developing the team
- Running effective team meetings
- Recognising factors that motivate and de-motivate individuals.

## Why is team development important?

The manager's role in building a team is an on-going one. It is a common mistake for managers in our field to believe that once they have a complete team, they will all 'get on with it' and the manager only needs to think about the team as a whole again when someone leaves or extra staff are needed. However in our work things – and people – change all the time, and managers need to lead a group of individuals that can work together as a 'whole', constantly balancing the individual skills and qualities with the job in hand. Your most important asset is the people working for you, as how well they work together has a huge impact on the atmosphere of the setting.

# Developing your own skills

## Understanding basic theory on team traits and dynamics

No matter how small or large your staff team is, there are a number of roles that people play and responsibilities that could be allocated to each member according to skills, experience and personality. As you will know, personalities have a major impact on a team's dynamics. There are two theories regarding this that we think could help you and which we outline in brief below and we have given suggestions for further reading at the end of this book.

## The team traits theory

One of the best known theorists on team roles, whose work has been used in all kinds of management training and development, is Dr Meredith Belbin (2010). He studied team behaviour and structure for many years and he identified nine key roles that impact on teams working together. He recognised that we as individuals have a natural tendency to assume particular roles, called traits, according to our personality, our way of thinking and behaving. His research on the individual traits make interesting reading as he indicates the advantages and disadvantages of each. The nine roles/traits are: Completer, Coordinator, Implementer, Monitor/Evaluator, Plant, Resource Investigator, Shaper, and Team Worker.

## Dynamics of team development

The next theorist that you may find useful is B. W. Tuckman (1965), who studied and researched the way groups of people develop together. He analysed different stages of team development and labelled each stage according to what is going on:

- **FORMING** – Not yet a team but a group of individuals who are polite, cautious and uncertain of their role and purpose and the direction of the team.

- **STORMING** – Personal agendas are revealed, sometimes resulting in challenges to responsibilities and roles: people try to get to know what it is the team needs to do and who will do it.

- **NORMING** – The team establishes ways of working, sets patterns of working practice and levels of commitment and builds trust.

- **PERFORMING** – Getting on with the job, with sharing and supportive teamwork, the team is productive and able to meet objectives.

When the team is new or if a new member has joined the team, a manager's role is to support the *forming* stage. This may mean more 'hands on', more direction and supervision, friendly checking up on the situation and observation. When the team is at the next stage, *storming*, there can be confusion and distrust that causes conflicts in the team. Here a manager's role is to mediate, remain open-minded and consistent in their approach to all members of the team, and to find a solution with the team by being rational, producing facts if necessary. At the *norming* stage the team needs a manager to be the organiser and motivator to keep up the team's momentum. At the final stage of *performing*, the manager is a facilitator for new ideas, problem solving, personal and professional development and setting new goals or targets with the team, keeping them focused on achieving the vision, as well as providing positive feedback for the team's achievements (see Chapter 5).

---

### First person – supporting team development

I had to build a team for a new nursery, and had some staff that had worked at another of the chain's nurseries and some who were newly recruited. I decided to hold the first team meeting at the local park before the nursery opened, and we played a number of games and did some fun tasks where they had to work out problems together. It got the two lots of different staff working together and seems to have got them through some of the 'forming' stages by helping them to get to know each other a little.

Nursery Manager

---

## Identifying your team's strengths and weaknesses

A manager could start by taking a look at their team as a whole and asking:

- What are the team's strengths and weaknesses?
- How does each member of the team contribute to these?

By capitalising on strengths you can develop skills, enthusiasm and team spirit. If you have an enthusiastic and motivated team working with you, the atmosphere is good, the job becomes more rewarding and people enjoy coming to work. Adults and children respond to the 'atmosphere' in child-centred settings – and how the team works together and gets along will be a major contributory factor to this. New ideas are generated because people feel they are heard and valued and the beneficiaries of all this are, of course, the children and families to whom you are providing a service.

Once you have reflected on your team as a whole, you can then start thinking about strengths and weaknesses in more detail by asking yourself such questions as:

- Do all your team understand their roles and responsibilities? This is different to just knowing the tasks and doing them.
- What have you done as a manager that would help individual team members get the full picture of what the team is there to do?
- Does your team have the chance to both give and receive regular feedback? (see Chapter 5).

- Is this feedback given freely and openly or are some people holding back information and experience?

- Does your team communicate openly and supportively with each other?

- Are they open to change?

- Who and what has influence on the team and their performance? For example, does the day-to-day physical environment influence the team, or are there particular staff members who are 'conspicuous by their absence'?

## Developing the team

Once you have thought about strengths and weakness of your team, you can use some of the following methods for developing individuals within the team:

- Match tasks to team roles until skills develop and then offer a chance to change.

- Hold regular team meetings and send the agenda around the week before for comments to encourage input to the meeting.

- Ask if staff want to have a 'roving' chairperson at team meetings, so everyone gets a chance to chair and develop skills.

- Train the team together, rather than sending them on courses one by one.

- Hold individual supervision sessions weekly or fortnightly to support new skills or practice.

- Make sure you treat everyone as part of the team, including the person that 'just does the snacks' or 'just does the escorting'.

- Think about improvements to the working environment that would help to build morale, such as painting the staff room or installing a water machine – even cheaper options such as putting up coat hooks can make a big difference!

- Deal with any underlying issues that may cause conflict straight away rather than wait until things get out of hand.

- Set clear, achievable targets and let the team know how you will support them in achieving them.

## Effective team meetings

Team meetings are an important opportunity for a manager to receive feedback, keep staff informed, get an update on how things are going, and explore ideas.

One of the problems that many managers of settings have is finding the right time and location for these meetings. It may be that you have to be creative and book some space in the local café or coffee shop to hold the meeting. This may entail people working in their own time and you need to decide whether this is appropriate. Can you offer recompense in some way, such as leave in lieu, or payment? You will also need to bear in mind confidentiality issues – discussing individual children in public places can be inappropriate.

Be prepared for the meeting. Circulate a draft agenda to all attending, and ask for comments and suggestions. If you have anyone coming from outside the setting to the meeting, be sure to state this in the agenda. Remember we often need a change of communication medium at team meetings – which are predominantly talk – to take in additional information. Visual diagrams, photos, videos if applicable, etc. all add to keeping up the learning and the momentum of the meeting. Remind staff the night before that the meeting is going ahead and at what time.

It is important that managers ensure the following:

- keep to the time and encourage others to do so;
- welcome anyone new to the team;
- ask for someone to take notes;
- discuss each item on the agenda and ensure that all have an opportunity to speak (even the quiet ones);
- do not let meetings drag on over the time allocated;
- use alternative methods of managing a team meeting.

## First person – developing team meetings

Team meetings were becoming really boring – the same people spoke every time and ideas were lacking, so the whole thing just ground to a halt half way through every time and motivation levels to attend and take part were at an all time low. I thought about the fact that people communicate in different ways and wondered how I could use this to help liven up meetings. So I put together a collection of resources – DVDs, catalogues, magazines, CDs, flipchart paper and big markers, even pictures and flash cards – and I began to use at least one type of resource at each meeting to spark discussion or to enable quieter members to give their feedback in different ways. Sometimes we'd watch a DVD about some sort of practice issue and discuss it in small groups afterwards, other times we'd use postcard pictures to talk about ideas for redesigning one of the rooms for example. Not only did we get better discussions and ideas, but the staff also got to know each other better as a result, so it had a great effect on team morale as well.

Playgroup Leader

## Motivational and de-motivational factors

It is generally understood that most people will share some motivational factors regarding work, added to which will be individual reasons for work and personal aims. Kenneth Blanchard (2004) says of motivation, 'Most people are enthusiastic beginners...I think people only lose their commitment when they realise that good performance does not make a difference.' Managers can maintain staff motivation if they understand that the common factors for all of us hinge very often on their own actions and behaviour.

Common factors that motivate people include: money, job satisfaction, status, recognition, security, responsibility, and meeting a need within the community. One or two of these factors have little relevance to work in our field as often the pay is not high and job security cannot be guaranteed. However, a manager will need to bear in mind that individuals do want recognition but not all want responsibility. In general people want to be paid on time and for the work they do and to feel that their work is worthwhile, even if what they do is not fully understood by the wider community.

Depending on what motivates individuals in your setting from the above list, the following suggestions may be helpful in improving motivation:

- goals that are achievable and/or teach new skills or understanding;
- promotion or career opportunities;
- being able to learn something new regularly;
- being part of a responsive and effective team;
- being needed;
- being able to use personal skills and knowledge;
- having a regular job with hours that suit personal commitments;
- doing something that is different every day.

## Case study

Hafiz has just taken over a small nursery with five staff, two of whom had been at the setting for six years. He realised that there was no meeting area for the staff, no regular system of appraisal and very little motivation in the team. He worked out a rota of weekly supervision with each member of the team and held team meetings once every three weeks. He then allocated part of the large entrance area as a staff meeting place and placed screens to divide the area off, with comfortable chairs for the staff. Another member of staff felt motivated enough to bring in a few posters to put up and they all helped in making a notice board for their meeting area. Through the supervision sessions Hafiz was able to check that people understood their roles and responsibilities and that they knew they were able to attend training courses relevant to their work, and he gave them all an area of responsibility in the nursery within their own capacity and interest.

## Things that lead to people feeling demotivated

Things which de-motivate an individual will be those factors which work against whatever motivates them. These might include:

- an individual's lack of understanding about their role in the team;

- no induction into the job and the team, resulting in not knowing what they are there to do;

- no meetings to allow concerns and issues to be raised;

- lack of commitment by other members of the team;

- workload too demanding and/or long hours;

- lack of responsibility;

- lack of recognition for work done;

- not being involved in major decisions that affect them or that they have specific expertise in;

- managers being unfair – saying one thing and doing another;

- managers not acting on staff members' concerns;

- personality clashes and conflict in the team leading to an unpleasant atmosphere.

By showing staff how their job fits into the overall vision of the setting and giving them opportunities to take part in the decision-making process, you will build on the effectiveness and overall success of the team. However, you will also need to deal with those issues that cause unrest in others, such as an individual team member being unreliable or showing no real commitment to the job. The other members of team may consider it unfair if you do not attempt to find a solution to these issues, which, of course, may include dismissal.

## Rewards

Rewards are a way of keeping motivation high. In our field financial rewards are not always possible, so if this is the case, managers need to get creative and it may be that the following ideas will help:

- praise, if genuinely conveyed, is always welcome because we all like to be told we have done well (see Chapter 5);

- thank-yous, giving thanks by sending a card that others have signed as well;

- giving a gift such as a book, flowers, vouchers;

- promotion to another job, or the next level, or to other tasks that require more responsibility;

- allocating an extra day's holiday for commitment;

- arranging a treat for the whole team, such as a day out, lunch brought in for them, a night out together, or cream cakes for all!;

- free uniform.

Rewards must be fair; if one individual has obtained a reward so must another be able to. If it is for the whole team then the whole team must be able to benefit from it or enjoy it, e.g. do not give an ordinary birthday cake to someone who cannot eat gluten. In giving rewards make them public and personal. If giving a box of chocolates to each member because of their hard work during the year, do not leave them in the kitchen with labels on them – instead give them personally to each team member with a 'thank you' and a smile! Recognition is important to how we feel about ourselves; the reward is not just the chocolates, it is your personal recognition of the individual. 'Many things affect confidence – even a few simple words' (Landsberg, 2003).

## Putting it into practice

- Be clear about what you are saying to your team, what it is you expect of them and what they can do.

- Ensure that you do not confuse your team by saying one thing then doing another.

- Look at how you are managing the team; you cannot expect to be trusted and respected just by having the title 'Manager'.

- People like to have control over their responsibilities; give them room to develop their own skills by allowing them this control.

- Bring everyone together informally from time to time to learn more about each other and the work.

- Never leave a new member of staff to do their own introductions; always make them welcome and expect that they will be nervous and unsure at first and need support.

- Do not rush in to dealing with all conflict issues; some resolve themselves. However, if an issue amongst the team is affecting the children at the setting and/or others in the team, raise this concern with those involved.

- Do not favour one member of the team, however well you get on with them.

- Remember that as a manager you oversee how the team gets the job done; it is your responsibility to help individuals understand where their job fits into the overall picture and vision of the setting.

# Evaluation processes

Managers who regularly review the practices and programmes in their setting will recognise that evaluation helps to keep practice and procedures in line with the vision of the setting as well as ensuring that the setting is up-to-date and offering the best possible service to children and families. Good practice and quality are not assured just because a setting has met all the needs of the children. Managers of settings need to think ahead, as well as look at what has been happening before. Carrying out an evaluation process will enable a manager to do this in a structured and meaningful way. However well your setting is running, as a manager, it is important to work from the assumption that every setting can be improved in some way.

## Essential skills for carrying out evaluation

- Understanding the tasks of a manager
- Choosing a method
- Planning, collecting and analysing data
- Getting others involved
- Dealing with successes and failures.

## Why are evaluations important?

We believe the purpose of implementing an evaluation process is to look at the whole (or part) of the setting to see if the aims and objectives are being met. This is important as it is very easy for everybody to get very involved in the day-to-day routines of the setting and not notice that practice or legal requirements have moved on, or indeed that the children currently in the setting have different needs from those attending last year. Carrying out formal evaluations helps managers to take a step back from routine operations and to think about the development of the service for children and families.

# Reviews and evaluations

Teams which hold regular discussions about current issues in the setting – for example, what to do about the cleaning of the centre, how best to welcome a new child who has specific needs – can be said to be regularly reviewing their practice. If done openly and fairly, these reviews will help the manager to keep on top of issues that can be dealt with fairly easily. A review would be held after a specific incident or to address an immediate need, whereas an evaluation would include how the service deals with such incidents overall or investigate how or why certain needs had arisen in the first place and/or were dealt with. Evaluations enable managers to learn from what has happened in the past and implement new practices as a result of this in line with the aims and objectives of the setting.

# The evaluation process

There are many different models of the evaluation process and depicting it as a circular process helps us to think about the importance of learning from reflection when carrying out any piece of evaluation work. For example:

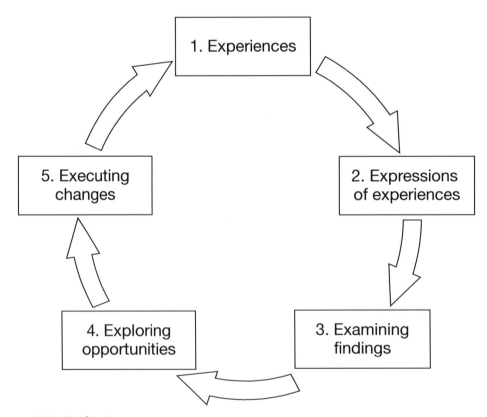

**Figure 10.1** Evaluation process

1. The 'experiences' stage refers to the children's or adults' experience of the service and the provision of different aspects of the setting

2. 'Expressions of experiences' refers to comments of the children and staff in a variety of ways according to their own interpretations of what they have felt, enjoyed, or not enjoyed about the various aspects of the setting and the programme

3. 'Examining findings' is where the team and/or manager look carefully at what has been said or discovered

4. 'Exploring opportunities' is the stage whereby new ideas and opportunities for change are examined

5. 'Executing changes' is where the suggestions and comments made as a result of the evaluation are put into practice.

## First Person – evaluating resources

We had a summerhouse in the garden and it was supposed to be for children to use for their play. However, recently it had got used as a storage area and a 'general junk' place, and the children didn't use it much. We asked the children about how they used the summerhouse and how they would like to use it. The team then discussed the ideas that came forward, and after exploring all the practicalities, we decided to try different ones out each week. We then asked the children to tell us about their experience again after a month to see which ideas worked and which hadn't.

After-school club Manager

# Developing your own skills

The way the manager implements the process will have direct implications on the quality of the feedback. It is important not to look for 'scapegoats' or 'heroes/heroines' in the process; evaluations must remain open and focused on the aims of the evaluation, rather than being set up to find out who's to blame for something going wrong, for example. The skills identified in this section provide a framework for identifying the necessary priorities and appropriate action to follow when carrying out an evaluation process.

# Understanding the evaluation process

1. To set up the process and to ensure that it allows all who are connected with the setting to play a part in the evaluation

2. To record and analyse the findings of the evaluation

3. To draw up an action plan, based on the findings, and implement it.

# Methods of evaluation

There are a wide variety of methods used in evaluation processes and some are used alongside each other.

The second stage, 'expressions of experience', can be easily carried out with your team by using a SWOT analysis, a method often attributed to Albert Humphrey. Managers should decide which aim/objective(s) they want to evaluate and then ask team members to do a SWOT analysis on how they feel this is being achieved. SWOT is an acronym for:

- **Strengths**
- **Weaknesses**
- **Opportunities**
- **Threats**.

A SWOT analysis can be done in one of two ways:

**Formally:** asking staff to complete a form that has each of these words on it and a gap underneath for comments. The benefit of this method would be that individuals could give their thoughts and opinions on equal terms. On the other hand, there would be no debate or discussion.

A series of questions such as the ones below could be used when thinking about how we are working to achieving this aim/objective:

- What do you think our strengths are?
- What do you think our weaknesses are?
- How can we build on our strengths?
- Are there any opportunities we have missed?
- What do you think the threats to achieving this are?

**Informally:** Having a team meeting or a series of team meetings looking at each of the four areas of the SWOT process and recording the feedback on a flipchart or through note-taking. The benefit of this method would be to encourage everyone to discuss and debate and check what views are realistic and which are not, although some staff may feel that they do not need to join in the discussion.

Whether done informally or formally, by doing a SWOT analysis with your team you should be able to get a clear picture of how people feel that their work in a particular area is progressing and issues that need to be addressed. This can then lead you into the last two stages of the evaluation process.

## Case study

As manager of a playgroup, Clarise wanted to see if she could get more children and their parents/carers to attend to achieve their aim of providing a community service. Clarise decided that they needed to start with a SWOT analysis to see how the rest of her team felt they were achieving this aim. She drew up the questions covering each of the four areas and gave a set of them to each member of the team so they could think about it and prepare for the next meeting. Meanwhile she looked through her records to see if there was any other information that could help, such as thank-you letters giving details of why parents used the playgroup, or complaints to say why they didn't! She then contacted the local authority to see if there were any new schemes being set up in her area and gathered other local information that might help her with the evaluation process, such as numbers of children in the area.

## The Who? What? Why? Where? When? method

### Who?

Who is involved will depend on what it is that is being evaluated. For example, if it is an objective of the baby room in a nursery which is being considered, then there will probably be very little point in involving staff from other rooms, unless of course you are evaluating how the transition from one room to another is experienced by children. However, if you are evaluating whether the overall aim of the setting is being achieved, then it is important to involve as many people as possible, including parents and children.

Managers should remember that being part of an evaluation process can be an invaluable learning and development opportunity for some members of staff, as not only will it encourage them to develop their reflective practice (see Chapter 3), but it will also enable them to understand how their daily work contributes to the whole (and this of course may be a motivational factor for some people – see Chapter 9).

### What?

Exactly what you decide to evaluate will depend on the following:

- the aim and objectives of your setting;
- what you are hoping to use the results of the process for.

> ## Case study
>
> Joanna, manager of a full-day care scheme including an after-school club, wanted to find out about their usage of the new building. The goal of the evaluation was to use this data as evidence of continual improvements and for the basis for further funding applications.
>
> She drew up a list of questions which covered all the things she wanted to find out about all of the areas of the new building, including the outside area; who used them, when and how often. She then looked at how she would get this data from everyone. Questionnaires could be used for staff and could be followed up with a focused team meeting to discuss findings, but the children would not find that method very easy or enjoyable. So she asked the staff to come up with some activities that would get feedback from the children. They designed a game where children moved around based on Joanna's original questions and a member of staff recorded the information.

## Why?

Evaluations can be driven by internal events, such as managers wanting to check progress with a particular project, or external events, such as funding applications which require input from children and parents. Managers need to set out clearly the purpose of any evaluation process and to make sure that they only collect and analyse data to achieve this evaluation (rather than the one you wished you were doing or realised you should have been doing half way through!).

## Where?

Most of the work that involves gathering of experiences and data will take place at the setting, but not all. Managers may carry out a fuller evaluation of a holiday playscheme after it has taken place somewhere other than the venue. This would allow both those who attended the scheme and those who worked there to have more time to reflect on all the aspects before giving their ideas or opinions. Annual General Meetings (AGMs) and parties or open days can be useful opportunities to gather experiences of parents and other supporters and agencies. Some managers take their teams away from the normal working environment, allowing them to benefit from being in a different place which can create an atmosphere which promotes reflection and discussion.

## When?

Evaluation processes should take place as often as possible and be a routine part of a manager's workload, rather than a quick question-and-answer action that gets looked at once and then locked away in a drawer so the quality assurance action plan can have a tick by 'evaluate your service'! Depending on what is being evaluated and how, the frequency of evaluation will differ from setting to setting, but managers should probably be routinely thinking about evaluation if they are not actually doing it!

# Planning, collecting and analysing data

This part of the exercise may take some time, especially in reflecting on issues to be included and in planning the action points. It is important not to underestimate the amount of time you will need for the process to take place if you want it to be successful!

## Planning

The following points will need to be considered:

- what the goal of the evaluation is;
- the range of questions to be asked;
- who is to take part and when;
- how the process will work – which methods to use;
- what the deadline is or what other time constraints will impact on the exercise;
- who will see the results;
- how the results will be used.

## Doing

- brief staff and children about the process;
- capture peoples' views and experiences;
- collect other relevant information, e.g. facts, numbers, policies etc.

## Analysis

- draw up a grid or table to record findings from each method used to collect data;
- check you have as much data as you need or whether you need further information;
- clarify with those involved any points or issues that are not clear;
- study the findings to find out whether they answer your original questions and what those answers appear to be;
- decide how to present your findings and write up the results of your evaluation.

# Putting it into practice

- Incorporate evaluation as a regular part of your role as a manager.
- Look at what areas/issues have been coming up in team meetings that might suggest that a formal evaluation is necessary.
- Give plenty of warning to the team that this process is going to happen and explain what the purpose of it is.
- Ask children to be involved where appropriate and be creative in enabling them to do so, and remember to let them know about the results.
- Plan your evaluation and remember to allow plenty of time to do it properly.
- Make sure you implement the findings to avoid evaluation becoming a pointless exercise!

# Further reading

Adair, J. (2009) *Effective Leadership: How to be a successful leader.* London: Pan Books.

Adair, J. (2011) *100 Greatest Ideas for Effective Leadership and Management.* Oxford: Capstone.

Adair, J. and Allen, M. (2003) *Concise Time Management and Personal Development.* London: Thorogood.

Ashman, C. and Green, S. (2004) *Self Development for Early Years Managers (Managing in the Early Years).* London: David Fulton Publishers.

Aubrey, C. (2011) *Leading and Managing in the Early Years.* London: Sage Publications Ltd.

Back, K. & Back, K. (1999) *Assertiveness at Work: A Practical Guide to Handling Awkward Situations.* Maidenhead: McGraw-Hill Book Company.

Belbin, R. M. (2010) *Team Roles at Work.* London: Butterworth-Heinemann.

Berne, E. (1996) *Games People Play, The Psychology of Human Relationships.* London: Penguin Books.

Blanchard, K., Zigarmi, D. and Zigarmi, P. (2004) *The One Minute Manager – Leadership and the One Minute Manager.* New York: HarperCollins Entertainment.

Cavanagh, M. (2003) *Against Equality of Opportunity (Oxford Philosophical Monographs).* Oxford: Clarendon Press.

Clemments, P. E. and Spinks, T. (2009) *The Equal Opportunities Handbook: How to Recognise Diversity, Encourage Fairness and Promote Anti-Discriminatory Practice.* London: Kogan Page.

Coleman, M. and Glover, D. (2010) *Educational Leadership and Management: Developing Insights and Skills.* Maidenhead: Open University Press.

Daly, M., Byers, E. and Taylor, W. (Eds). (2009) *Early Years Management in Practice.* Harlow: Heinmann.

Dickson, A. (1982) *A Woman in Your Own Right: Assertiveness and You.* London: Quartet Books.

Doran, G. T. (1981) 'There's a S.M.A.R.T. way to write management's goals and objectives', *Management Review,* 70 (11), pp35–36.

Douch, P. (2006) *It Doesn't Just Happen: Inclusive Management for Inclusive Play.* London: KIDS.

Fisher, K., Rayner, S. and Belgard, W. (1995) *Tips for Teams: A Ready Reference for Solving Common Team Problems*. New York: McGraw Hill Professional.

Fisher, R. and Ury, W. (2003) *Getting to Yes: Negotiating Agreement Without Giving In*. London: Random House.

Fleming, I. and Hailstone, P. (2003) *The Time Management Pocket Book*. Alresford: Management Pocketbooks.

Gillen, T. (1997) *Assertiveness*. London: Chartered Institute of Personnel and Development.

Heller, R. (1998) *How to Delegate*. London: Dorling Kindersley Ltd.

Heller, R. and Hindle, T. (1998) *Essential Managers Manual: Vol. 1*. London: Dorling Kindersley Publishers Ltd.

Hersey, P. (1984) *The Situational Leader*. Chichester: John Wiley & Son.

Hopson, B. & Scally, M. (2009) *Build your Own Rainbow: A Workbook for Career and Life Management*. Chalford: Management Books 2000 Ltd.

Hughes, B. (2001) *Evolutionary Playwork and Reflective Analytic Practice*. London: Routledge.

Jay, R. (2002) *How to Build A Great Team*. London: Prentice Hall

Johnson, D. W. and Johnson, F. P. (2008) *Joining Together, Group Theory and Group Skills*. Harlow: Pearson Education.

Jones, C. (2008) *Leadership and Management in the Early Years: A Practical Guide*. Oxford: Oxford University Press.

Kapasi, H (2002) *Playing in Parallel: A Study of Access to Play Provision by Black and Minority Children in London*. London: London Play.

Landsberg, M. (2003) *The Tao of Motivation: Inspire yourself and others*. London: Profile Business.

Lindenfield, G. (1986) *Assert Yourself*. London: Thorsons.

Lindenfield, G. (1992) *Assert Yourself: A Self-help Assertiveness Programme for Men and Women*. London: Thorsons.

Maitland, I. (1999) *Managing your Time*. London: Chartered Institute of Personnel and Development.

Malik, H. (2009) *A Practical Guide to Equal Opportunities*. Cheltenham: Nelson Thornes.

Moyles, J. (2006) *Effective Leadership and Management in the Early Years*. Oxford: Oxford University Press.

Newstead, S. (2006) *The Buskers Guide to Anti-Discriminatory Practice*. Eastleigh: Common Threads Publications Ltd.

Newstead, S. (2009) *The Big Buskers Guide to Leadership*. Eastleigh: Common Threads Publications Ltd.

Paige-Smith, A. and Craft, A. (2007) *Developing Reflective Practice in the Early Years*. Maidenhead: Open University Press.

PIP Guidelines Series 1. (2002) *It Doesn't Just Happen*. London: Kidsactive.

*Pocket Oxford English Dictionary* (10th edition 2005) Oxford: Oxford University Press.

Reed, M. and Canning, N. (Eds.) (2009) *Reflective Practice in the Early Years*. London: Sage Publications Ltd.

Robins, A. and Callan, S. (Eds.) (2008) *Managing Early Years Settings: Supporting and Leading Teams*. London: Sage Publications Ltd.

Siraj-Blatchford, I. and Manni, L. (2007) *Effective Leadership in the Early Years Secto*r. London: Institute of Education.

Smith, A. and Langston, A. (1999) *Managing Staff in Early Years Settings*. London: Routledge.

Taylor, G. (2000) *Managing Conflict*. London: Directory of Social Change.

Tuckman, B.W. (1965) 'Developmental sequence in small groups', *Psychological Bulletin*, 63, 384–399.

# Contact list

### Chartered Institute of Personnel and Development

Tel: 020 8612 6200 www.cipd.co.uk

The institute supports and promotes management, personnel and training, and is an awarding body for some qualifications.

### Child Care Monthly

http://info.childcare-magazine.com

Child Care is a monthly magazine which provides vital information, special features and practical activity ideas for childminders, nannies and other professional childcarers.

### Children and Young People Now

www.cypnow.co.uk

Children & Young People Now magazine provides a service to managers and senior practitioners working with children, young people, and their families.

### Children's Legal Centre

Tel: 01206 877 910 www.childrenslegalcentre.com

The Children's Legal Centre is a unique, independent national charity concerned with law and policy affecting children and young people.

### Children's Play Information Service

Tel 020 7843 6303  www.ncb.org.uk/cpis/home.aspx

An information resource service specialising in children's play.

### Common Threads

Tel: 02380 629460 www.commonthreads.org.uk

Common Threads is a world-wide community of playwork practitioners, trainers, development and support workers, authors, academics and theorists which promotes playwork theory and practice.

## Community Insight

Tel: 01249 447146 www.communityinsight.co.uk

Community Insight specialises in professional development for people who work with young children.

## Free Play Network

Tel: 07790 981175 www.freeplaynetwork.org.uk

The Free Play Network is a network of individuals and organisations, which aims to promote the need for better play opportunities for children.

## Fields in Trust

Tel: 020 7427 2110 www.fieldsintrust.org

An organisation that specifically supports the use and improvement of playing fields, playing spaces and playgrounds for all children.

## Institute of Leadership and Management

Tel: 01543 266867 www.i-l-m.com

Provides tailored support for leaders and managers at all levels.

## KIDS

Tel: 020 7359 3073 www.kids.org.uk

KIDS is a charity with a number of programmes for disabled children and young people.

## Kidscape

Tel: 020 7730 3300 www.kidscape.org.uk

An organisation that researches, lobbies and provides resources on bullying, child protection and generally keeping safe.

## Letterbox Library

Tel: 020 7503 4801 www.letterboxlibrary.com

Specialists in non-sexist and multicultural books for children.

## National Children's Bureau

Tel: 020 7843 6000 www.ncb.org.uk

A national organisation that supports, researches, lobbies and advises on all aspects of children's lives.

## National Childminding Association (NCMA)

Tel: 0845 880 0044 www.ncma.org.uk

Work with registered childminders, nannies as well as other individuals and organisations to ensure families have access to high quality home-based childcare, play, learning and family support.

## National Society for the Prevention of Cruelty to Children (NSPCC)

Tel: 020 7825 2500 www.nspcc.org.uk

Produces literature and training courses relevant to working with children.

## Nursery World

www.nurseryworld.co.uk

Produces a weekly magazine and other services.

## PlayBoard Northern Ireland

Tel: 028 9080 3380 www.playboard.org

PlayBoard are involved with the creation and implementation of new initiatives and projects. They are all aimed at the common goal – 'Changing the child's world through play'.

## PLAYLINK

Tel: 020 7720 2452 www.playlink.org

PLAYLINK is a multi-faceted independent play and informal leisure consultancy working in the areas of design, planning, policy, strategy, local engagement, fundraising and organisational development.

## Play*words*

Tel: 02380 629460 www.commonthreads.org.uk

Play*words* publishes playwork theory and practice, with the specific aim of supporting new and academic writing in the playwork field.

## Play England

Tel: 020 7843 6300 www.playengland.org.uk

Play England works to give children and young people in England regular access to free, inclusive, local play provision and play space.

## Play Scotland

Tel: 0131 440 9070 www.playscotland.org

Play Scotland works to promote the importance for all children and young people, and campaigns to create increased play opportunities in the community.

## Play Wales

Tel: 029 2048 6050 www.playwales.org.uk
   Works to raise awareness of children and young people's need and right to play.

## The Children's Society

Tel: 0207 841 4400 www.childrenssociety.org.uk
   Defends, safeguards and protects the childhood of all children.

## The Daycare Trust

Tel: 0845 872 6260 www.daycaretrust.org.uk
   Daycare Trust is the national childcare charity which promotes high quality affordable childcare for all.